Grow A Happier Healthier Lifestyle

The Happiness Tree

Learn How to Be Happier

Your Guide to a Path of Increased Happiness and Health

By
Dr M.A Smithard

Acknowledgements

The author has drawn from many sources but is particularly indebted to the following authors whose work has heavily influenced and informed this book:

Yuval Noah Harari *'Sapiens A Brief History of Humankind'*

Ajahn Jayasaro *'Without and Within'* and other books and videos on Buddhism

Thanissaro Bhikku *'The Bhudda's Teachings, An Introduction'*

Prof Mark. W. Muesse *'Practising Mindfulness:An Introduction to Meditation'*

Amit Sood M.D *'The Mayo Clinic Handbook for Happiness'*

Prof Tim Spector 'the Diet Myth, the True Science Behind What We Eat'

Chris Woollams *'The Rainbow Diet'* and many other books and resources

The author wishes to thank his family and friends for their encouragement and support. He is particularly grateful to David Hindley, David Wilson and Peter Findlay, for their detailed review and edit of the manuscript and their valuable suggestions for improvement. He would like also to acknowledge the encouragement he received from valuable discussions with Daniel and Jamie Griffin, Rosemary Smith, Ken Smithard, Ron Smith and Ray Jones. He wishes to thank Jo Jo Griffin for the cover design image, and Roy and Chris Smithard for support with website and IT. Last but not least, he wishes to thank his wife for putting up with him during this time.

CONTENTS

Introduction

Purpose

The primary purpose of this book is *educational,* though it is in part also *exploratory.* **The primary aim** of this book is to make the reader aware of the many and varied factors that can have a **positive impact on your happiness and health**. The book draws together a wide range of material to give the reader an overview of the subject as well as pointing the way to detailed resources and training material. In this way it aims to act as a *self-help* book that guides the reader to a path of *increased happiness and health.*

Most of us will say that *above all else* we want to be *happy*, though we're often not clear on exactly what happiness is, nor how we can become happier. It's not obvious, and we don't learn about it at school. We do however know that we have to earn a living, and we know that money can help solve many problems. So, we get on with our lives and defer thinking about happiness till later; we treat happiness as a future destination.

To learn more about happiness, we might ask questions such as:

What is happiness?
Is happiness a natural state for humans?
How much is our happiness predetermined by our genes?
How much is it determined by our upbringing and experiences?
How much is it determined by our present lifestyle and circumstances?
How much is it determined by our brain chemistry?
How does our thinking affect our happiness?
What can we do to become happier?
Where can we learn more about it?

This book aims to present you with knowledge that helps you to answer these questions, together with suggestions on how to use that knowledge to increase your own level of happiness.

Most of us also rate good health high up our wish list but may have lifestyles that don't promote good health. This book presents you with suggestions on how to make healthier lifestyle choices. Our minds and bodies are very closely connected, so too are our happiness and our health.

Our mind/body is complex beyond understanding. But if we could make best of use of the knowledge that is available, to become happier and healthier, then that would be useful. There is a vast wealth of such knowledge spread over many specialist disciplines and cultures, spanning human history. It is an **objective** of this book to extract, summarise and bring together relevant parts of that existing knowledge into one place, to make it more accessible to the reader.

The nature of the subject is complex and intertwined. Some of it is "fuzzy" in nature, so it's not easy to get to grips with, and the terminology and context is varied. It is therefore a **further objective** to present the summarised information in a novel, user friendly way that that makes it is easier to navigate, understand, learn, and remember.

There is a **secondary aim** to this book, which is to produce something that may have *wider application* and be of interest to teachers, trainers, academics and specialists in the various subject fields. For example, if the material could be made into a structured form, then it might serve as a complete "map" of the subject field, so that other more detailed sources, knowledge, and training material could be cross-referenced to it in a systematic way. If the material could be made sufficiently modular and compact then it might more manageably be verified, improved and used as an educational tool.

These aims and objectives are ambitious, which is why the book is in part *exploratory.*

Individual readers find their own ways to read a book, but the author has suggested a few ideas in Part 5 that he hopes might be helpful.

The Method Used

The author has explored a wide range of factors that are believed to have an influence on our happiness and health, and the many resulting methods which are claimed to make us happier and healthier. He has attempted to identify the level of evidence that supports the claims.

Relevant information has been drawn from a wide range of disciplines including: Evolutionary Theory, Anthropology, Buddhism, Mindfulness, Psychology, Psychotherapy, Medical Science, Health, Fitness and Nutrition. Collectively it's *"more than a brainful"*, yet it's relevant to us all. The information has been extracted, condensed and then rearranged into one single **multidiscipline** source and arranged as a **hierarchical structure** to make it easier to access and navigate.

The world, our evolution, our bodies, brains, minds, thoughts, emotions, behaviour, and relationships are interactive and complex beyond present understanding. It's not surprising that our attempts to describe in words what we learn are sometimes a bit woolly or entangled. In addition, this field necessarily includes some intangible, fuzzy, concepts like "happiness", "self ", "mind" and "thought", that are difficult to express in words. Therefore, it seemed like a good idea to add **pictures, analogies** and **quotations** to the book to promote understanding. This has resulted in three original models, *The Happiness Tree, The Happiness Cup* and *The Mind State Model.*

The author has also taken the liberty of modifying and adding to the source material in places. This has been done in an attempt to clarify, bridge gaps, make cross connections, and harmonise the material so that the parts best fit together in the models. The intention has been that, as a teaching aid, the total might become more than the sum of the parts.

(Note: for those interested, more information on how and why this book was written is provided at the end in the Afterword)

Part 1. The Happiness Tree Model

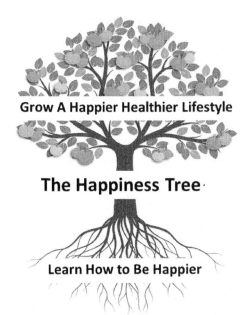

Figure1.1

1.1 The Happiness Tree Analogy

The Happiness Tree Analogy is shown above in Figure 1.1

- The roots of the tree represent your choice to learn how to be happier, your education in happiness, and the roots of your inner happiness.
- The branches of the tree represent your lifestyle, and the choices that you can learn to make in order to grow a happier and healthier lifestyle.
- The smaller sub-roots and side-branches represent progressively more detailed educational and training material (structured text).
- The rising sap, which nourishes the branches of the tree, represents the generic knowledge and wisdom that you draw from the roots and learn to apply in your everyday life.
- The trunk represents the strength and resilience that you gain from cultivating your mind and body so that you can bend with the wind.
- The leaves represent your access to resources, learning material and to other people.
- The fruit of the tree represents the help, support and knowledge that you give to others to help make the world a slightly better place. This fruit represents your legacy.

1.2 How this Book is Structured

In Figure 1.2 we show how the happiness tree model is structured into a hierarchy of roots and branches. Each root or branch has an associated "chapter" in the book. The words " choose " and " learn " are deliberately chosen and deliberately repeated for emphasis.

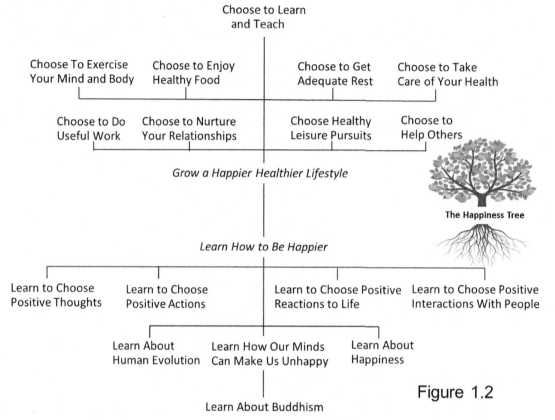

Figure 1.2

The text associated with the roots and the branches is a mixture of educational and training material. The educational material explains what to do and why and explains the benefits. The training material gives tips on how to actually do it.

You might say our minds and our lives are too complex to fall into a simple structure like this, and that's true. On the other hand, many of us learn and remember more effectively if the information is structured and associated with a picture.

The information in the associated chapters splits down into ever increasing levels of detail, like the roots and branches of a tree. The model is thus hierarchical, so that at the top layer you can view the complete field of information with relatively few words. You can then 'drill down' to lower layers to reach detailed paragraphs and sentences of text.

As you start to read the book you will automatically become more familiar with the structure, but just to start you off there are a few notes below that you may want to look at.

Each root/branch is designated by letter and number as shown in in Figure 1.3 below. This notation is then reflected in the associated text, as chapter, section and paragraph headings, as shown in Figure 1.4. below. You can access the material at any level, in any order. More sub-branches and sub roots can be added as needed.

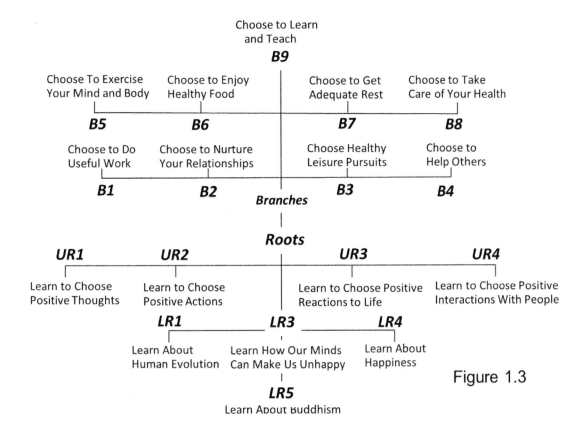

Figure 1.3

Figure 1.4 below shows how the model is structured. For example, UR1.1 is a sub-section of Chapter UR1, dealing with the subject of Learning to Meditate.

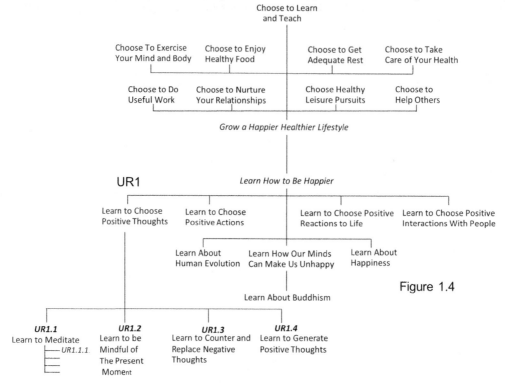

Figure 1.4

.1.3 The Roots: Our source of Inner Happiness

The Roots contain educational information from which you can learn about happiness, as well as techniques that you can learn to increase your level of happiness. This information has been drawn from several disciplines and then combined in a particular way.

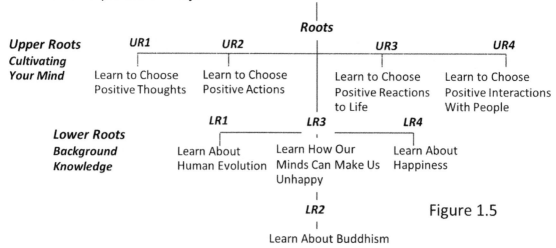

Figure 1.5

The Lower Roots, LR1-4, contain *Background Knowledge* drawn from various disciplines including *Evolutionary Theory, Buddhism, and Psychology.* They also contain some *ideas* that have been added by the author. You will be able to explore some aspects of the human condition, to understand what *happiness* is, and to identify the many factors that affect it. The material in these lower roots is intended to be just sufficient to give you background knowledge and provide context to the overall model.

The Upper Roots, UR1-4, deal with the process of learning to *Cultivate Your Mind* to generate *Inner Happiness*. Here you will learn about techniques that you can practise to gradually increase your level of *inner happiness*. These techniques work by changing the way you think about things and enabling you to make more positive choices. Information has been drawn from *the Lower Roots* and other sources. The author has taken the liberty of interpreting and synthesising that information and re-structuring it in a particular way that is aimed at making it easier to understand, learn and remember.

1.4 The Branches: Our Lifestyle Choices

The branches of the tree represent your lifestyle. They have been chosen to reflect recognisably different aspects of everyday life (work, rest, play, family etc.) in a structure that is also consistent with the roots of the tree. The lifestyle choices that you make, directly affect your happiness and health (and in some cases your wealth). The branches include activities that are your external sources of happiness (job satisfaction, positive relationships, pleasurable pursuits, etc.).

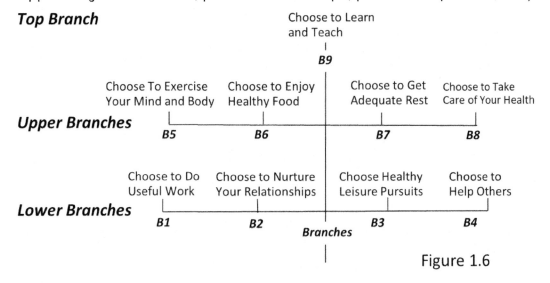

Figure 1.6

The Branches have been split into levels for ease of presentation, as shown in Figure1.6.

The Lower Branches B1-B4 are as follows; B1 addresses work, B2 relationships, B3 leisure and B4 helping others.

The Upper Branches B5-B8 have a common theme relating to lifestyle choices that help maintain your *health and wellbeing*. B5 is about exercise and development including mind- body practices, B6 is about eating healthily, B7 is about Rest and B8 is about various aspects of protecting your health.

The Top Branch B9 is about learning and teaching.

The Happiness Tree

You may wonder why health related choices are shown in a lifestyle intended to build happiness.

The first reason is that while good health does not in itself make us happy, sickness can make us very unhappy. So inner happiness is all about thinking but a healthy lifestyle helps.

There's a second reason. When we get sick, we usually go and consult a doctor or other health professional. They are highly trained, highly motivated, and do a fantastic job. They perform miracles every day, but their resources are not boundless. We also have a part to play. It's our responsibility to stay as healthy as we can by making sensible lifestyle choices.

We all must die. The object of choosing healthy lifestyle options is not about trying to live forever, but rather to remain healthy, active, and happy for as long as we can. Who wants to be sick?

There's a third reason. Scientists are finding that the brain and body are very much more closely connected than previously supposed. You will find an overview of this in DVD (Digital Video Disc) *"The Connection"* by Shannon Harvey. For example, food and exercise can affect our mood and anxiety levels. Some of the many other connections are referred to within the *branches* because of their relevance to health and happiness.

1.5. Important Differences Between the Roots and Branches

The roots and the branches represent education in two different dimensions of our lives. The generic knowledge learned from the roots UR1-4 can be applied throughout the day, in whatever lifestyle activity we are engaged in (thinking, working, playing etc.). It can also be used to help us balance the branches of our lifestyle by influencing our choices.

For example, what we learn in UR4 about positive interactions with people can be applied in almost every branch; in B1 with work colleagues, in B2 with family relationships, in B3 with friends we spend our leisure time with, in B4 with those we try to help, in B5 with those we meet in the gym, and in B9 with those we teach, or learn from.

Similarly, the generic moral undertaking to try to avoid harming the environment (part of UR2) can be used to influence many of the lifestyle choices that we make (for example, our job, how we travel, what we buy, what leisure activity we choose, how we manage our house etc.).

The educational material in the branches is more topic specific. It can help us to make positive choices to enhance our lifestyle (like healthy eating). It can also include training on how to implement that choice (learning to cook healthy food).

This tree model makes a distinction between *inner happiness* (addressed in the roots), and *external sources of happiness* (which comes from activities in the branches).

1.6. A Simplified Tree

There is necessarily great duplication between the lower and upper roots. You can read the lower roots for background, then once they have served their purpose, you can choose to discard them like boosters from a rocket (or think of them as scaffolding that was initially needed to build the tree). You might then choose to remember a simpler version of the Happiness Tree that results, as shown in Figure1.7 below.

On the other hand, you could choose to look more deeply into original authentic sources of the lower roots. It's up to you.

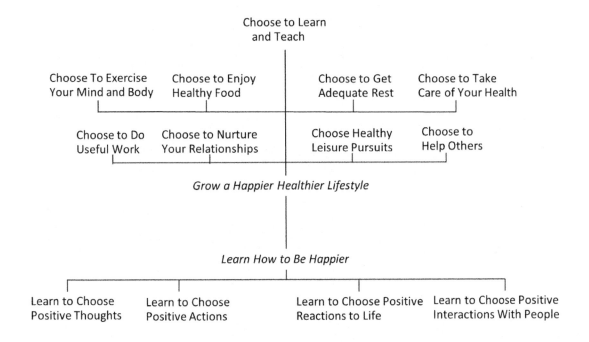

Figure 1.7

Part 2. The Lower Roots; Background Knowledge

Introduction

The Lower Roots contain *Background Knowledge* drawn from various disciplines including *Evolutionary Theory, Buddhism, and Psychology.* They also contain some *ideas* and *new models* that have been developed by the author. The material in these lower roots is intended to be sufficient to give the reader background awareness and provide context to the overall model.

LR1 deals with human evolution, LR2 is a brief overview of Buddhism, LR3 is concerned with the psychology of how our minds can make us unhappy, and LR4 explores the many different factors that determine our levels happiness.

(Many themes in this book have been drawn from Buddhism and Mindfulness. The section LR2 is therefore extensive in order to acknowledge their source).

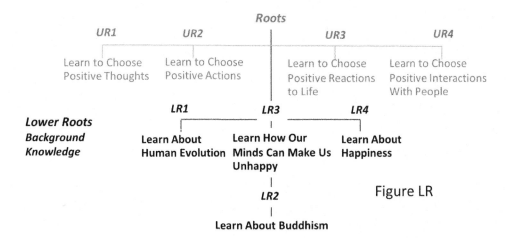

Figure LR

LR1 Learn About Human Evolution

Introduction

In this section we learn just a little about human evolution. Specific topics have been selected that give background and context to our present-day condition, and yield inferences for our present happiness and health. Our knowledge comes from the fossil record but supported by anthropological studies of the few remaining hunter gatherers that survive. For those who want to learn more read *"Sapiens A Brief History of Humankind" by Yuval Noah Harari*, which provides an excellent overview.

For those of you who are religious and don't believe in the theory of evolution, you can skip this section. You could think instead about how our creator formed us to thrive in the natural world and the capabilities that our creator formed in us.

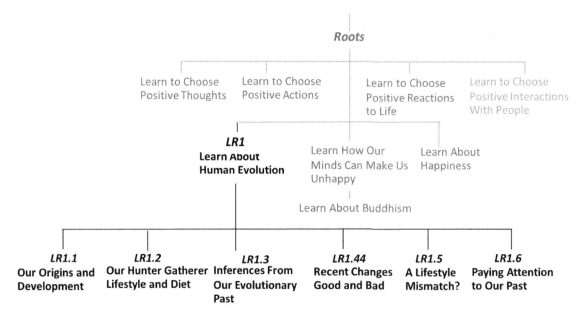

FigureLR1

LR1.1 Our Origins and Development

Land animals and plants first emerged on earth about 500 million years ago, and dinosaurs about 245 million. The first primates (monkeys and apes) emerged around 55-85 million years ago. We inherit much of our genes/DNA from them and from earlier species. For example, we inherited the essential survival instinct to behave in such a way as to get a pleasure reward (food, drink, warmth, comfort, sex).

Modern humans evolved from an ape like ancestor very slowly over a million years or so. The first fossils of modern man (*homo sapiens)* that have been found are around 300,000 years old.

Early *homo sapiens* co-existed for a period with other, now extinct, human species including *Neanderthal* (some of whose DNA we retain).

We evolved in many ways. We developed enhancements to previous capabilities, but also acquired new features. There were physical changes to our body and brain. Our diet also changed (about 3.5 million years ago) from the predominantly leaf and fruit diet of other primates to a more mixed diet (calacademy.org>science news Andrew Ng Jun 4, 2013, Early Human Diets).

We developed a more upright stance, bigger brains and developed increased manual dexterity. We lost our keen sense of smell but developed vocal chords.

We learned to make fire and to cook. We were then able to more easily chew and digest a wider range of foods. There is evidence that humans were cooking energy rich carbohydrate vegetables 170,000 years ago (A McNamara 03 Jan 2020 sciencefocus.com>news). This led us to evolve a smaller intestine, and freed up more time for other activities. Most importantly, cooking is thought by scientists to be one of the primary factors that contributed to the development of our larger brain.

We also developed the ability to create stereotypes of perceived threats, and to react immediately and instinctively to them, so as to increase our chance of survival.

We developed a stress reaction. When we perceive a threat, our brain switches us briefly into a superhuman mode; our blood gets a surge of cortisol, our pulse quickens, we get stronger and our brain speeds up, we are then ready for fight or flight.

Our brains evolved not just by getting bigger, but also by the addition of new parts. The parts of our brain that control bodily movement have much in common with those of primitive animals like snakes. Other parts that deal with emotional responses and body language are not much different from the corresponding part of a dog's brain (which may be why humans and dogs can read each other's body language and get on so well). The later part of the brain that humans developed, (the cortex) is different from those of most other creatures and deals with language and the many conceptual thinking tasks such as logic and rational thought.

Our improved brain enabled many new, complex processes to take place. We developed good memories, abilities to compare, to recognise patterns, to analyse, to model and to predict and communicate. These abilities would have improved our ability to track and hunt as well as being aware of seasons and terrain for gathering food.

Our large brain made childbirth more difficult, so humans are born not fully developed and require years of parental care. This led to long term pair bonding, and made the need for group support a very strong one. It also meant a longer period of learning/teaching and conditioning of the child so that it could survive and become a useful member of the group.

Our improved brain allowed us to think creatively. This together with physical changes that increased our manual dexterity led to our learning to make tools and flints, to make clothing from skins, to make shelters, to light fires and cook. We also domesticated dogs for hunting and security, and learned to make traps, to fish and to make boats. These advances made us more efficient at getting food and may have freed up time for leisure and social activity like dancing, singing, telling stories, and making art and ornaments, as well as pondering our place in the universe.

There were other less tangible, but very important, advances which followed the development of language and communication. We learned to communicate abstract ideas such as rules, morals, conventions, and agreements. This allowed humans to cooperate in larger groups as well as helping with trade, and eventually led to civilisation.

The ability to pass on acquired knowledge by practical teaching, orally, and by images will have been an important factor in accelerating progress. It's sometimes called *Cumulative Knowledge*.

LR1.2 Our Hunter Gatherer Lifestyle and Diet

We are thought to have existed as small, isolated groups of hunter gatherers. Anthropologists can draw some indications of how our ancestors lived by studying the lives of hunter gatherer groups living today.

The common stereotype of early man is of a violent club wielding hunter cave man who ate mostly meat, but anthropology shows a different picture. Looking at present day indigenous people seems to show that meat is only a small part of their diet (possibly because of unavailability or difficulty of catching game). Herman Pontzer studied the *Hazda* people in Tanzania and the *Ache* in Paraguay. In his book *Burn* he concluded that their diet consisted of about fifty percent meat and fifty percent vegetable, supplemented by honey.

When excavating ancient human habitation sites, animal bones are commonly the most obvious indicator of what early humans ate, because they are more likely to be preserved than the remains of plant-based food. But scientists do nonetheless find cooked, charred remains of nuts and seeds, (and even wild grass seeds), so the fossil record is not inconsistent with the results of anthropological studies. Further evidence of the plant component of our early diet is found by scientific analysis of the human bones.

As humans migrated, they had to cope with varying climates and conditions and survive seasonal shortages of food. They evolved the ability to survive on a wide range of foods. Our anatomy, particularly the teeth and the intestines, confirms that we are omnivores (*Dr McArdle 28.07.21 Biology Online*). The actual diet of our ancestors.(*bbc.com>news>health Recreating the caveman diet P Roxby 17 Sep 2010*). would have varied according to location and season, but it is generally thought to have included a mixture of fruit, nuts, seeds, roots, and wild vegetables. Some carb rich roots *rhizomes* and *honey* are thought to have been an important food source because of their high calorie content. Protein may have been obtained from birds, eggs, fish, meat, shellfish, amphibians, and grubs. It's thought that some groups developed genetic changes that allowed them to cope with a specialised and restricted diet (eg the *Innuit*, the *Masai*, and nomad *Mongol* herdsman).

Our microbiome (gut bacteria) will have evolved with us.

To help avoid harmful food we developed a mechanism whereby, if our brain doesn't recognise the appearance, taste and smell of a potential new food, it "tells" us that we don't like it.

At some point humans found that if they lived near the sea or a lake, then they had a year-round source of food. Living near the coast would have meant a diet high in fish and hence in omega 3 oil which is an important brain nutrient. It is thought the earliest modern humans migrated out of Africa and very gradually moved along coastlines, via the Middle East to Europe and along the Southern coast of Asia eventually reaching to the East and to Australia. They developed some genetic changes such as eye and skin colour as part of adapting to cold climates. Despite this, modern humans all over the world are the same species, the genetic variations are small.

We can only conjecture at the level of intra and inter group violence that existed amongst the earliest humans. Given their very low population density and lack of "ownership" of territory, it may be that they had more to gain by cooperation than rivalry (intermarriage, trade, sharing knowledge). Some studies support this but others suggest the opposite, that we learned to turn our hunting weapons on ourselves at an early stage.

LR1.3 Some Inferences from Our Evolutionary Past

We can use what we have learned about our millions of years of evolution to make some inferences about our present condition; -

- Evolution didn't design us to be happy, but to survive. Therefore, it's not surprising that we may need to learn to be happy, that it may not just come automatically.
- Given that our brain is made up of different bits, it's not surprising that we can sometimes feel a conflict between our rational mind and our emotional response, especially when making decisions.
- Evolution favours diversity within a species, so it's not surprising we're all so different (including our levels of happiness).
- We evolved as mutually supporting social animals, so it's not surprising that isolation makes us unhappy, nor that altruism is instinctive, nor that helping others makes us feel good, nor that we enjoy teamwork.
- An isolated hunter would have had less chance of survival, so being a group member was very important. Expulsion could mean hardship or death. It's not surprising therefore that we value approval and respect from our peers. Nor that we mostly conform to the group customs or norms, to reduce friction or violence within the group.
- We had to form strong bonds and relationships to survive and to procreate and raise children, so it's not surprising that successful relationships and family life are important human needs and contribute to our sense of well-being, nor that we like to spend time developing and maintaining our social bonds. It's also not surprising that we sometimes behave tribally.

- We probably had to work hard to get food and shelter and survive, so it's not surprising that we need activity and get unhappy if we're idle for too long. And it's not surprising that exercise makes us feel good.
- It's not surprising that we like being in natural environments, near water and trees.
- Many people seem to have an instinctive craving for carbohydrates, sugar and fat, presumably because their high energy content was an aid to survival.
- It takes a while for us to get to like a new food.

LR1.4 Recent Changes, Good and Bad

The development of farming is thought to have started some 10,000 years ago. This included the cultivation of cereal crops to make bread and the domestication of animals for meat and dairy. The land could then support more people. The increasing population led to the development of bigger communities, settlements, then towns and cities. Then city-states, kingdoms and empires formed.

This birth of civilisation led to the development of writing, which allowed much greater cumulative knowledge to be acquired. It also led to mathematics, science, medicine, engineering, technology and the arts, and widespread trade by land and sea. Various forms of religion emerged. Our conditioning, through education became more intensive, and more varied as different cultures evolved.

However, the many benefits of civilisation came at a price. The centralisation of power led to big gaps between rich and poor and to widespread poverty. Close packed communities were vulnerable to contagious diseases. Crop failure led to starvation. Inter-state rivalries led to large scale warfare and to the taking of slaves. Many people had replaced a hunter gatherer lifestyle for a life of drudgery in some form of specialised work.

Although all the same species, the widely different cultural and educational influences conditioned humans in different regional groups to behave differently. This sometimes led to conflicts (and still does). These differences due to cultural conditioning appear to be greater, but less visible, than the genetic or racial variations.

It is an interesting question to ask whether the hunter gatherer was healthier than the farmers or city dwellers of the emerging civilised world? There have been hints from archaeology that the hunter gatherers lived longer than did the first civilised people. Studies of the life expectancy of present-day hunter gatherers show that they live about as long as the rest of us even without access to medical care, and despite a higher infant mortality rate. This suggests that our ancestors may have lived healthier and longer lives than the civilised people that followed them.

We could also ask if our hunter gatherer ancestors were happier than their civilized descendants? According to Yuval Harari this is an important question that has largely been ignored by historians and anthropologists. We have tended to believe that the march of progress that made 20th century man more affluent, healthy, and happy than medieval man, must always have been moving onwards and upwards. We have therefore tended to assume that modern man must be happier than our early ancestors, who we imagine struggling to survive in a frightening and savage world. But those who have looked have found strong indicators to the contrary. Anthropologist James Suzman has written a book *Affluence Without Abundance* in which he records his experiences of living for 25 years among one of the few surviving hunter gatherer peoples, the Kalahari Bushmen in Namibia. He reports that they live entirely in the present moment, focused on satisfying their immediate needs (which are few). Their skills as hunters and food gatherers mean that they can acquire their food readily and have adequate leisure time to spend with family and friends and on hobbies. He also found that they have a different concept of time, and see time as cyclical (days, seasons, years) rather than linear as we do. They don't have our concepts of history or progress and so spend no time worrying about the future or the past. He suggests that although their life was not without problems, they were generally happy. He relates their happiness to the same kind of experience that we can enjoy when we are absorbed in the present moment, in purposeful activities such as a long trek, dancing, creative crafts, or writing.

LR1.5 A Lifestyle Mismatch?

Farming and civilisation didn't start till about 10,000 years ago, that's only a one hundredth part of our evolutionary period of 1,000,000 years. Evolutionary changes are very slow, we have changed very little in 10,000 years. We are basically the same as our hunter gatherer ancestors. For example, we have not all yet fully adapted to the introduction of wheat and dairy into our diet 10,000 years ago, so some of us are intolerant to these foods.

We haven't changed much, but our world and environment has changed massively, and the pace of change is increasing ever more dramatically. Many of us now live busy stressful lives, in close packed cities, remote from the natural environment, getting little exercise, often eating abundant but poor-quality food. We seem to be increasingly suffering from diseases such as diabetes, Alzheimer's, heart disease and cancer. We spend more time worrying about the past and the future and spending little time in the present. Some of the very qualities that made us successful as hunter gatherers can, in our present environment be distorted into negative mental traits such as greed, jealousy, perfectionism and over-working. Our lifestyle can become out of balance, and our stress reaction overused. We are told that globally, stress related diseases and mental illness is increasing.

It seems then that this *"mismatch"* between the environment that we evolved in and our present one could be a major cause of ill health and unhappiness. We are living in an environment, and in a way, that our evolutionary past has not prepared us for. We weren't 'designed' for this. Yet mostly we are blissfully unaware of this possibility, we feel that our condition has been continuously improved by "progress".

How can we *escape* from the consequences of this *"mismatch"* ? We can't go back to being hunter gatherers. We can't wait for our evolution to "catch up" because it's too slow. What else can we do?

This book is not intended to be a rant against the evils of progress, nor a lament for a lost paradise of natural living. Rather the author's intention is to see what lessons we can learn from our past and examine ideas that might help us *escape* from this *mismatch*. Can we find a way to lead happier, healthier lives, by somehow *adapting* to the present environment. Can we in this way get the 'best of both worlds'?

(If you like acronyms, think APE Adapt to the Present Environment, or ESCAPE Evolutionary Short Cut to Adapt to the Present Environment).

Globally, there is another mismatch. Our species has been so successful that we have over-populated the world, driven other species to extinction, and polluted the planet enough to threaten our own future existence. We have learned to exist reasonably harmoniously in progressively larger groups, but war continues to be a problem. Some populations lack democratic freedom, some suffer genocide and suppression. We have not yet found a way to reach the required international/global agreement to solve these problems. This itself appears to be the most serious single problem in the world. Evolution has made us extremely adaptable, maybe we will find a way to solve it?

LR1.6 Paying Attention to Our Past

We often find ourselves in need of information to make an informed choice. Science usually provides that information and the evidence to support it. But there are sometimes questions that science can't answer definitively. For example, if we ask, "which diet is best for our long term health?", science gives us many strong indicators (for example the benefits of the Mediterranean diet). But to conclusively *prove* which is the healthiest possible diet, would require a vast trial using thousands of people in many countries over a period of say 50 years. That's not practicable. In such a case, we can use evolutionary science to give us an indicator. If we do that, we might conclude that eating the natural diet, that we ate for a million years or so, is likely to be better than any other because it's what we evolved on and are adapted to.

We can use evolutionary theory in this way, as a "litmus test", to check many other propositions put to us regarding our lifestyle and health. It isn't guaranteed to be 100% accurate but when trying to ponder otherwise unfathomable but important questions, it can help. And it's likely to be more reliable than solutions put forward by those with a vested interest. For example, we could explore what sort of urban environment and housing suits us best, what sort of exercise, what sort of lifestyle, what sort of socio-politico-economic system?

LR2. Learn About Buddhism.

Introduction

This root gives a superficial introduction to Buddhism. The author's intention is not to preach Buddhism, but to show where some of the strands of thought in this book have come from. This section is intended to provide background and context to the Happiness Tree, and to show how it has been derived: (material has been extracted from Buddhist and other sources, reformatted, and structured to form the upper roots of the Happiness Tree, which is thus rooted in Buddhism). For a deeper understanding of Buddhism, you may wish to study some of the more authoritative sources signposted in the resources section.

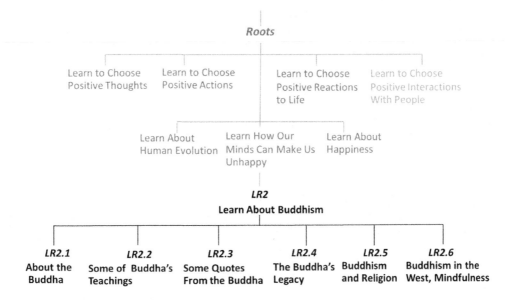

Figure LR2

LR2.1 About the Buddha

The *Hindu* religion was prevalent in India more than 5000 years ago. The associated discipline of *Yoga* was also widespread. It included spiritual and moral themes and meditation, as well as the mind body practices (asanas) which have recently become popular in the west. Siddhartha Gautama, the man who later became known as the Buddha (the enlightened one) was born into this Hindu and Yogic culture in 623 B.C. in the gardens of Lumbini in what is now a region of northern India.

    Although born a prince into a wealthy family, Siddhartha Gautama was very conscious of the human suffering he saw around him, and the inevitability of old age, sickness, and death. He saw that life in many ways seems unsatisfactory. He asked himself three questions.

    1 is there a way to find a happiness that can overcome this suffering and dissatisfaction and even transcend death?

The Happiness Tree

2 if so, can this happiness be found through human effort?

3 if so, can it be found in a harmless and blameless way?

Then he gave up his luxurious lifestyle, left his wife, child, and family, put on the robes of a mendicant holy man, and set off on a mission to find the answer to his questions. During his 8 years of wandering, he tried various solutions, including severe asceticism and various forms of meditation. His approach was to try something, observe the effect, and if it didn't work move on and try something else. Finally, one morning, after he had meditated for twelve hours under a tree, he found that the answer to all three questions was *yes*; he became the *Enlightened One*, the *Buddha.*

When he became enlightened, he had discovered a process for achieving happiness. But he realised that what he had discovered seemed so much outside normal human experience that it would be difficult to explain it. He also realised that it would be difficult to prove that his discovery was *"true".* He chose instead to teach his followers the process or path by which they could make the same discovery for themselves. Many of his followers then achieved enlightenment for themselves, experienced extreme happiness, and helped spread the word.

The Buddha spent the rest of his life teaching others how to learn some of what he had learned. His teaching spanned 45 years. His lessons were delivered orally, and re- transmitted orally, by his followers. His teachings, the *Dhamma,* were later recorded in the Sanskrit language. He also formed a monastic order, the *Sangha,* to preserve and propagate his teaching. The Buddha realised that most of the people he taught would be unable, because of their livelihood and family commitments, to devote themselves to the path of enlightenment as fully as those who became monks. He nonetheless encouraged his lay followers to believe that they would get significant benefits in proportion to the effort they made, and some lay followers achieved the first stage of enlightenment.

Buddhists talk of having the *Triple Gem,* that is the *Bhuddha,* (the enlightened one) the *Dhamma,*(his teachings) and the *Sangha* (the monastic order that studies, practices, and spreads the teachings and so maintains the order).

LR2.2 The Buddhas Teachings (The Dhamma)

Buddha had many profound philosophical insights into the nature of the human condition, His thinking spanned philosophy, psychology, moral ethics, interpersonal relations, and community life. Many Buddhist teachings are concerned with the process of cultivating our minds to achieve *inner happiness.* Other teachings are more outward looking and aimed at promoting *social harmony.* Some aspects of his teaching are summarised below, largely using translation from the traditional terminology of the Southern or Theravadin tradition of Buddhism.

LR2.2.1 The Four Noble Truths

1 There is suffering, (Dukkha) life seems unsatisfactory.

2 There is a cause of suffering, and it is rooted in our everyday thinking (e.g. attachment to material things, grasping, failure to see life as it really is).

3 An end to suffering is possible when it's causes (grasping etc.) cease.

4 There is a process we can use to achieve that end, a path to follow.

There is a duty implied by these truths; to understand the nature of suffering and its dependence on clinging to certain activities or feelings, and to understand that craving is the cause of suffering.

LR2.2.2 The Eightfold Path

This is the process that Buddha taught to bring an end to suffering. It represents 8 parallel strands or parts of the path that we should try and follow as part of our everyday lives. It is sometimes represented as a circle with the 8 smaller circles mounted on the outside of the circumference (like strands of a cable).

1 Right View
2 Right Thought (resolve, intention)
3 Right Speech
4 Right Action
5 Right Livelihood
6 Right Effort
7 Right Mindfulness
8 Right Concentration

Right View

Refers to seeing things as they actually are. It includes belief in the human capacity for improvement / enlightenment, and it includes understanding the law of Kamma, (that our past and present actions determine our present and future state and condition).

Right Thought (resolve, intention)

This refers to being resolved to hold thoughts consistent with Right View, to abandon toxic thoughts (such as cruelty, hostility, harm, greed and hedonism) and aspiration to be free of inner affliction. It also includes the intention to have thoughts of kindness and compassion.

Right Speech

Refers to true, useful, and timely speech that is polite and of kindly intent. It involves abstaining from lying, harshness, slander, deception, divisive speech, and idle chatter.

Right Action

Refers to actions that do not harm self or others. It includes abstaining from killing, stealing, illicit sex and substance abuse (these, together with not lying, are also called the 5 precepts).

Right Livelihood

Refers to livelihood that does not cause harm to self or others and is not dishonest. (for example the wrong livelihoods listed include selling drugs, weapons, people, and poisons).

Right Effort
Refers to an endeavor to eradicate existing unskillful (negative) thoughts, emotions and toxic mental states and prevent new ones arising. It also refers to fostering existing skillful (positive) thoughts, emotions and mental states and introducing new ones. For example, unskillful thoughts include mindless worrying about the future, and toxic mental states include greed, jealousy, and materialism. Right effort is motivated by the desire to end our craving which is the cause of our unhappiness.

Right Mindfulness
Refers to keeping in mind and maintaining an awareness of the present moment, in terms of the sensations of the body, the nature of the experience (pleasant, unpleasant, neutral), the state of one's mind and mental phenomena that may arise, without reference to their meaning in the context of the outside world.

Right Concentration
Refers to *Jhana*, what we mostly now call meditation. There are two levels of Jhana meditation. The first *Samatha* is aimed at calming the mind. We now call it *single point focus meditation* or *attention-based meditation*, usually concentrating on the breath. The second level is *Vipassana*, translated as Insight Meditation which is aimed at gaining insight into our thoughts and traits. *Right Concentration* provides the nourishment to allow *Right View* and *Right Thought* to do the work of ridding us of craving and toxic mental states.

The *Eightfold Path* is sometimes split into 3 subdivisions instead of 8 and called *Triple Training*.

> The first two, Right View and Right Thought come under the heading *Discernment*.
> The next three, Right Speech, Right Action and Right Livelihood come under the heading *Virtue*.
> The final three, Right Effort, Right Mindfulness, and Right Concentration come under the heading *Concentration*.

(Note that some of the content of the Eightfold path is not necessarily in tune with current thinking in many cultures, for example the references to abstaining from illicit sex and selling weapons).

LR2.2.3 The Three Perceptions or Insights

The *Three Perceptions* were provided by the Buddha to serve as tools to help us understand more fully the four noble truths. They are also explored during *insight* meditation practice.

1 Inconstancy. (Anicca) This refers to the fact that everything in life is impermanent and transient (including life itself) and that transient things are unreliable sources of happiness.

2 Suffering. (Dukkha) This refers to the fact that life is permeated by suffering and dissatisfaction.

3 Not Self (Anatta) This concept draws attention to the fact that we cling to a concept of self that is not real. We do not have a permanent unchanging self.

LR2.2.4 Stages of Enlightenment

The Buddha taught that there are stages of enlightenment, that represent progressively higher levels of attainment. Some laymen can reach the first level. The higher levels are reached by only a small number of monks. (Note; these more advanced aspects are beyond the scope of this book).

LR2.2.5 Some Buddhist Themes

Here are some *themes* that seem, (to an inexpert eye), to be part of Buddhist teaching. (As an individual you can choose to agree with them or not).

- All humans want to be happy
- We experience life through our senses, then generate perceptions and thoughts and feelings from these sensations. We attach meaning or existence to the object or events perceived, but things may lack the inherent existence that we attach to them.
- All things are interdependent. For example, everything we do affects others and vice versa; most of us cannot exist without the support of others.
- We tend to attach a notion of permanence to things that we don't perceive to be changing rapidly. Lack of acceptance of impermanence (and one's own impermanence) leads to unhappiness.
- We have a strong sense of self, but we change according to our conditioning. Attaching too strongly to our concept of self may lead to unhappiness.
- When not focused or engaged our mind wanders in a way that was likened by the Buddha to a monkey jumping around the branches of a tree *(the monkey mind)*. To develop inner happiness, we must calm our wandering mind and live more in the present moment.
- Our minds become conditioned by the stream of perceptions that make up our life experience, and we form negative traits (defilements) such as *greed, craving* and false concepts and beliefs such as *self, permanence*. If we grasp too tightly to these concepts and beliefs, then we become less happy.
- We also have to become *aware* that it is the *conditioning* of our mind that causes our unhappiness through the formation of negative traits and false beliefs. The Buddha taught that it is possible to change that conditioning, by a process of cultivating the mind. This process involves recognising and acknowledging the negative traits and false beliefs, and the harm that they cause to ourselves and others, then learning to gradually detach from them by practising meditation, mindfulness and compassion. He also taught that we have to believe that we are capable of changing that conditioning, and we have to be willing to undertake the process that enables the changes to occur and to assess our progress.

LR2.3 Some Quotes from the Buddha

On a subject as complex and intangible as the mind, it can be difficult to comprehend the meaning of particular words or teachings. Quotations can help. Here are a few quotes at random from the Buddha, they can help us see what the Buddha was "getting at". You will find links to more quotes below in *Resources*.

Do not dwell in the past, do not dream of the future, concentrate the mind on the present moment.

Nothing can harm you as much as your own thoughts unguarded.

The mind is everything, what you think you become.

We are what we think. All that we are arises with our thoughts. With our thoughts we make the world. All that we are is the result of what we have thought.

You only lose what you cling to.

Health is the greatest gift, contentment the greatest wealth, faithfulness the best relationship.

Peace comes from within, do not seek it without.

No one saves us but ourselves .....we ourselves must walk the path.

If we do not help others, who will help us when we need it?

A true friend is one who stands by you in need.

It is better to travel well than to arrive.

To be idle is a short road to death.

It is better to conquer yourself than to win a thousand battles.

Holding on to anger is like grasping a hot coal with the intent of throwing it at someone else; you are the one who gets burned.

Every human being is the author of his own health or disease.

Your work is to discover your work and then with all your heart give yourself to it.

LR2.4 The Buddha's Legacy

Gradually, after his death, the Buddha's teaching spread across many parts of Asia. Some different schools emerged as his teaching was translated and absorbed into the different cultures, languages, and religious beliefs of the various regions. There are therefore differences in the content of the various texts. Nonetheless expert scholars tell us that there is a consistency and coherence that points to a single source.

The *Theravadin* or Southern form of Buddhism that spread across Sri Lanka, Burma, Thailand, and neighbouring parts of Southeast Asia is thought to have been based on the earliest texts. The *Mahayana* or Northern school of Buddhism spread to Tibet, China, Japan and neighbouring regions and is said to be the largest Buddhist school. There is a third school *Vajrayana* mainly associated with Tibet, Bhutan, Nepal,and Mongolia. Buddhist sometimes refer to these three schools as being *"three turns of the wheel of Dhamma"*.

There is evidence that Buddhism also spread Westwards from India along the silk road. There is archaeological evidence of Buddhist temples in ancient Egypt around 400-500 BC. Buddhism also reached ancient Greece in around 300 BC probably as a result of Alexander the Great's eastern conquests, and Buddhism is thought to have had an ongoing influence on Greek culture.

Buddhism has survived 2500 years and has had a profound effect on the lives of the many people who live in Buddhist countries. In Thailand for example, Buddhism is an integral part of the national culture and has a strong spiritual influence on everyday life. Children start to learn about Buddhism at school. Most villages have a local temple which forms the hub of community life in each village, as well as being home for the monk. The community supports the *village monk* with gifts of food and other necessities, as well as helping with tasks to improve or maintain the temple. The village monks support the community by teaching, by giving advice to those who seek it and by carrying out services such as weddings and funerals and festivals on special days in the Buddhist calendar. They also work to maintain the temple buildings. The community and the monks work together to organize charitable fundraising events where visitors can get not only spiritual guidance from the monk, but also free food, music, and dancing. These events not only raise money to help provide for the needy, but also are part of the social calendar that helps bind the community together. Rich and poor alike regard it as important to make gifts to the temple and to those in need. This is called *Tambon*, it is part of the culture and people believe it gains them merit.

An aspiring Buddhist makes a choice to undertake a gradual process of training or cultivation of the mind, and endeavours to live morally and to show compassion to others. The benefit to the individual (inward looking) is an increased calmness, equanimity and happiness. The benefit to society (outward looking), is that if many people make this choice, then there is an increased level of social harmony and happiness. The degree of benefit depends on the degree of effort, perseverance; and skill of the aspirant as well as the skill of his / her teacher.

Novice monks serve a period of apprenticeship learning from more experienced monks. They spend part of each day learning and chanting the Buddhist teachings, as well as meditating and carrying out routine duties such as collecting alms, helping with ceremonies and maintenance of the temple. *Forest* monks live in communities further away from a village. They live even more austere lifestyles. They do not undertake the same sort of community duties but instead devote most of their time to meditation and learning from senior monks. A monk who attains a high level of teaching skills gains great respect and undertakes a duty to spread the teaching. Monks living today report deep feelings of inner happiness despite leading austere lifestyles.

The Buddhist teaching has the potential to improve all our lives yet is little known in many countries. Most of its messages are not part of school education (except in some Buddhist countries). Fortunately, there are various organisations across the world that are working to spread the word.

LR2.5 Buddhism and Religion

The Buddha was not a god, he was a mortal, albeit an exceptional and charismatic one (whose image and existence in some counties is revered with God like respect). Buddhism is arguably not a religion. The Buddha did not teach the existence of a *creator god*, nor *of Nirvana* or *afterlife*. (It is true though that in some regions the Mahayana tradition has combined with pre-existing Hindu beliefs such as a creator god and reincarnation, and some have referred to the 'sister traditions' of Hindu and Buddhism. Some Hindus are also Buddhist).

According to Thai Buddhist Monk *Ajahn Jayassaro*, Buddhism is better thought of as an education, and has more in common with science than religion. To be a Buddhist requires no belief in a god or an afterlife, or in anything except your ability to improve your life.

Buddhism is not in conflict with religion but has facets in common with most religions (such as morality and compassion). Buddhists tend to be tolerant towards the religious beliefs of others and tend not to impose their own teaching on others.

These are important points given that many people who might wish to learn about Buddhism may already have a religion or may be atheist and might be put off by any perceived religious connotation.

LR2.6 Buddhism in the West and Mindfulness

LR2.6.1 Buddhism in the West

Some western scholars, and later immigrants from China and Southeast Asia, are thought to have first introduced Buddhism to the USA in the mid nineteenth century. In the twentieth century Buddhism started to become established in the West, and more texts were translated into English and textbooks produced. Some earlier translations of Buddha's teachings into English can be difficult for a westerner to get to grips with because they are set in the context of the language, culture, thinking and religious beliefs prevalent in India 2,500 years ago. Also, there are differences in terminology and emphasis between the different Buddhist schools and therefore between the resulting textbooks. Some of the Buddhist concepts seem counterintuitive and difficult to understand.

Fortunately, many western scholars, and some westerners who became Buddhist monks in Asia, have studied the subject over many years and written books and teaching material that are much easier for westerners to understand.

As a result, Buddhism started to become well known in the west. There are Buddhist Societies that promote the teachings and issue free books. There are courses and retreats, as well as websites, apps, YouTube videos and CDs. The book *Buddhist Solutions for the twenty first century by P A Payutto* specifically addresses the relevance of the Buddhist messages today.

There has also been a surge of interest from scientists, psychologists and psychotherapists. One western monk (Matthieu Ricard) has been dubbed in the media as " the happiest man in the world " after being the subject of MRI scans showing unusual development of the parts of his brain that are known to be associated with happiness

LR2.6.2 The Mindfulness Tradition

Over the last forty or fifty years, one particular aspect of the Buddha's teaching has been extracted from its Buddhist (and any perceived religious) context and transferred into a western, science-based format, known generally as *"Mindfulness"*.

Mindfulness is concerned with our ability to live in the present rather than the past or future. It particularly refers to our ability to be aware of what our body's sensors are telling us at a given moment. The most widely used definition of mindfulness is the "operational" one proposed initially by Jon Kabat-Zinn; *"mindfulness is the awareness that arises from paying attention, on purpose, in the moment, non-judgmentally"*. Meditation and other techniques are used to enhance an individual's ability to be more mindful of the present.

Quoting from Wikipedia, some of the individuals who have contributed the most to the increased popularity of this movement include Thich Nhat Hanh, Herbert Benson, Jon Kabat-Zinn, Richard J Davidson, and Sam Harris. Herbert Benson is also known for his work in establishing the close connections between mind and body and the discovery of the 'relaxation response'.

Jon Kabat-Zinn is often referred to as the *'Father'* of this *Mindfulness Tradition.* He learned meditation under Buddhist teachers while a research student at MIT, then went on to study its application to medicine. He studied particularly the role of stress in mental illness and the use of Mindfulness to reduce it. He went on to become internationally famous for bringing mindfulness and meditation into mainstream medicine and society. He is Professor of Medicine emeritus at the *University of Massachusetts Medical School*, where he founded the famous *Mindfulness Based Stress Reduction Clinic* in 1979 (MBSR) and the and the *Centre for Mindfulness in Medicine, Health Care and Society* at the University of Massachusetts Medical School in 1995. His techniques have been widely applied for example to provide pain relief and to treat depression. His work is having ever increasing influence both in the US and internationally. His methods are being used in many US hospitals and clinics, as well as in some UK schools and in the NHS. His work has been wide ranging. He has published many books including two best sellers; *Full Catastrophe Living; Using the Wisdom of Your Body and Mind to Face Stress Pain and Illness (1991)* and *Wherever You Go, There You Are* (1994). Jon Kabat-Zinn actively promotes his message to international politicians to help solve the global problems we face in the twenty first century.

Eckhart Tolle is another internationally well-known spiritual teacher on this subject, and one of the most popular and prolific authors. He prefers to use the term *Presence* rather than *Mindfulness* and has approached the subject from a different direction. After a difficult early life and periods of depression, he experienced an intense, inner spiritual transformation or awakening, and a subsequent peace of mind which has stayed with him for the rest of his life. He became a counsellor to friends, passing on what he had learned. Though not religious he went on to study various religions, being influenced particularly by aspects of Buddhism, Hinduism, and Christianity. It became his mission to teach others how to achieve inner peace. He is best known for his first books The Power of Now. (1997), and A New Earth (2005). He went on to produce many more books, recordings and DVDs and set up *Erchardt Tolle Teachings* and *Eckhardttolle.com.* In 2008 he joined TV talk show host Oprah Winfrey for 10 live webinars which were subsequently accessed by 35 million viewers.

Mindfulness has been the subject of an explosion of interest in the west. There are very many books and other resources to learn from. Mindfulness is also the subject of a great deal of scientific research and extensive media coverage. Beginners may find the terminology confusing. The term *mindfulness* has come to be used more loosely as its popularity has grown and it seems to now be given a wide range of meanings that encompasses other aspects of Buddhism. The term is now widely used in advertising. The terms *mindfulness* and *meditation* are often used interchangeably in the literature, and used in combination, as in *mindfulness meditation.* In this book the term *mindfulness* will be used to describe the quality or ability of being aware in the moment. The term *meditation* will be used to describe the practice of a particular attention-based exercise concentrating on the breath. The two terms are thus *different* but *connected*, in that *meditation* is one of the (various) techniques that can be used to (among other things) develop *mindfulness*.

LR3 Learn How our Minds Can Make Us Unhappy.

Introduction

In this section we explore and reinforce the Buddhist theme, that our mind can make us unhappy in various ways, using knowledge drawn from Psychology. Some new original material is also added.

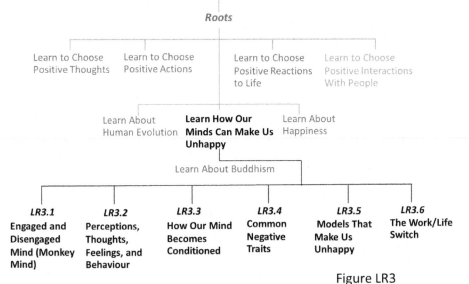

Figure LR3

LR3.1

Engaged and Disengaged Mind (Monkey Mind)

Although our minds are hugely complex, according to Amit Sood MD *(The Mayo Clinic Handbook for Happiness),* we can simplistically think of it as having only two states, *'engaged'* or *'disengaged'*.

When our mind is focused on some purposeful activity, for example, work, play, conversation or solving a problem, it is *engaged*. Usually in this state it is actively processing information from our sensors (vision, sound, smell, touch, taste) and carrying out actions in response to what it perceives. We can also be engaged when we are not paying attention to our sensors but are reflecting with a purpose, for example, trying to solve a problem. We tend to be happier in the engaged state and not easily distracted by random thoughts.

When our mind is disengaged it is not paying attention to our sensors and has access to the imaginary world. It has gone *offline*, but for no specific or immediate *purpose.* This seems to be the *default* condition when we are not occupied. In this state, while it is receiving no sensory input and has no directions, our mind seems to generates images and scenarios almost at random, from memory. These random scenarios generate random *uninvited* thoughts in response, likened by the Buddha to a monkey jumping around the branches of a tree *(the monkey mind)*. These thoughts can be positive or neutral or even creative, but they often instead tend to be negative, and they automatically trigger negative feelings that make us unhappy. We can become *lost* in these negative thoughts for long periods of time, but unaware of it. We are no longer in control of our mind, *"it"* has taken control of *"us"*. Often these negative thoughts are concerned with regrets of the past and worries about the future. We can become too concerned about the past and future and spend too little time in the present moment. Some of our negative thoughts may become habitual and keep returning to bother us. It's as though repeating them reinforces them (in a similar way that the preference algorithm in your phone's browser offers you the results of your recent searches). It's as though repetition makes them like a railway track that goes round in a loop. We then find it hard to get off the track to go somewhere else. We normally don't give much consideration to how our mind works, so we're not conscious of how these uninvited thoughts are constantly making us unhappy. Yet they can be very toxic, causing stress and anxiety. They can be a major source of our unhappiness. Later in the upper root UR1 we deal with techniques to combat them.

LR3.2 Perceptions, Thoughts, Feelings and Behaviour.

LR3.2.1 How We Perceive Things and Generate Thoughts
Psychologists study human behaviour and what influences it. Over time they have developed models of the process by which we experience the world and how we react to what we experience. Such a model is described below together with a picture analogy in Figure LR3.1.

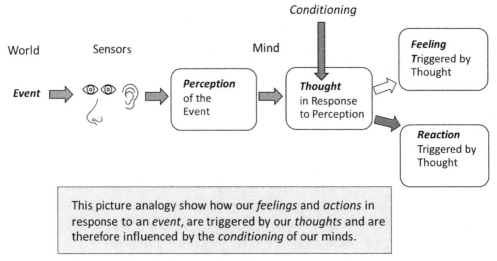

This picture analogy show how our *feelings* and *actions* in response to an *event*, are triggered by our *thoughts* and are therefore influenced by the *conditioning* of our minds.

FigureLR3.1

We *detect* objects, events in the world, and people, through our senses (vision, hearing, smell, taste, touch). We also receive communication this way.

Our brain interprets the information and forms a *perception* of the object / event / person / communication. We form a perception of what the "it" is that has been detected (the way this works is actually very complex).

We then generate *thoughts* in response to what we have perceived. The thoughts generated are dependent on how the brain has already been *conditioned or programmed* by previous experience. Different people can generate different thoughts in response to the same event.

The Happiness Tree

LR3.2.2 How Our Thoughts Generate Feeling and Behaviour.

When our mind generates a *thought* in response to a perceived *event*, that *thought* automatically triggers a *feeling* or emotion which may have a positive, negative, or neutral effect on our *happiness*. Thus, it is the thought that determines how we feel about an event, rather than the event itself.

The thought also determines our *reactions and behaviour* in response to what we have perceived. Thus, our *feelings* and consequent *reactions* are both determined by our *thoughts* about an event rather than by the event itself, and both therefore are dependent on our previous *conditioning* as shown in Figure LR3.1.

Our feelings determine our *present happiness*, and our actions and reactions have consequences for our own *future* condition and therefore our own *future happiness*.

We are part of the world and of nature, not separate from it. Our actions and reactions to events can have positive or negative *impact on the world.* We experience other people and their actions through our senses, and we form a perception and a thought in response to them. If the thought is a positive one it not only makes us feel happier, but it also causes us to choose a *positive interaction* with them. Positive interactions increase harmonious living and *make us all happier.* Conversely if the thought response is a negative one it makes us feel bad and is likely to cause us to choose a negative interaction. Negative interactions increase division, and can lead to strife, and further unhappiness.

In summary the *conditioning* of our mind has a major influence on our *happiness* and that of *others.* It can sometimes be the biggest *enemy* to our *happiness*. It follows that if we could change the conditioning of our mind and learn to choose more *positive thoughts, actions, reactions and interactions*, then we would be happier, we would make others happier, and the world would be a better place. It's not intuitively obvious how to do this, but there are various techniques and we will learn about them later in the *upper roots*. First, we start by examining conditioning in more detail.

LR3.3 How Our Minds Become Conditioned.

It is generally thought that some of our behaviour is instinctive and some the result of our conditioning. We instinctively have *aversions* to doing or thinking about things that make us *feel bad.* We seek instinctively to do things that give us *pleasure* (Freud).

Some things we learn by trial and error. We also have a built-in mechanism for learning by *penalty/reward feedback* (Pavlov's dog). It is thought that our mind becomes gradually conditioned by the *reward/penalty feedback* we get in response to our actions. In this way we learn *positive* or *negative habitual traits* depending on the feedback. We may learn to *share* or to be *selfish*, to be *mean* or to be *generous*, to be *honest* or *dishonest,* to be *kind* or *cruel.* There are many such habitual traits that are formed by our *conditioning.* Our conditioning is particularly important in childhood (*Shakespeare "the child is the father of the man"*). We can also be conditioned in other ways, for example by being influenced by others to believe which kind of behaviour is good or bad, or by continually repeating the same response.

It is thought that our mind is conditioned by the sum of our past life experiences. That includes what we learn in infancy from play, from our parents, from our education, from our work experience, from our peers, family, friends, from our culture, from our religion, from the media and from our direct life experience. It is plausible that we form some sort of vast knowledge base that we use to inform our thinking, our subsequent decision-making, and hence our behaviour. Hence our conditioning determines our behaviour, and in a sense determines, in part, *who we become*.(in part because both our genes and our conditioning have an influence: Nature v Nurture).

It is plausible that our mind forms various *models* of the world that can be used to help us survive and prosper. These models are also determined by our life experience and conditioning. These *models* largely determine the actions we choose (for example moral actions). They also determine our reactions to perceived events and our interactions with people. Some of these models we use to make quick judgements or comparisons, without the need for reflection. Others we can use more slowly and reflectively to analyse problems, predict outcomes, and make rational decisions. We can also assess the likely outcome of our decisions. This is particularly useful in our work. We also have many other models that we use to interpret life, and these also influence our thoughts and reactions.

In summary our mind becomes gradually conditioned by our life experience and it is this *conditioned* mind that determines the thought we have in response to a perceived experience partially through the action of habitual traits, and models. The resulting thought determines our emotional and physical response and hence our *level of happiness*, and our *behaviour*. We tend to be unaware of this. The conditioning of our mind has been gradual, it has helped us over the years to survive and prosper, it is deep seated, we feel it as part of who we are. We do not often look within, or question our long-held beliefs, nor face up to things we are averse to. We just get on with life as best we can.

LR3.4 Common Negative Traits

Here are some examples of learned habitual traits. You may like to reflect on how many others you can think of

Hate/Love, Greed/Moderation, Hedonism/Asceticism,
Selfishness/Generosity, Jealousy/Goodwill, Hostility/Empathy,
Prejudice/Tolerance, Cruelty/Kindness, Harshness/Compassion,
Rigidity/Flexibility, Deceit/Honesty, Fearfulness/Courage,
Pessimism/Optimism, Conceit/Humility, Ingratitude/Gratitude,
Malice/Forgiveness, Dogmatism/Openness.

We behave as though, for each trait, our individual *"setting"* can lie on a scale ranging from negative to positive. We may not be very conscious of our traits; others see them more clearly. When any setting is very negative then the trait can have a toxic effect. It causes us to choose negative actions, reactions and negative interactions with others and so generates unhappiness.

LR3.5 Models That Make Us Unhappy

Our models of the world serve a purpose to help us navigate life. But they are just perceptions of how the world is, they are not in themselves reality. Buddha taught that if we attach to them too strongly, or if we don't realise that they are just models, then we risk not seeing things as they really are, so making ourselves unhappy. Some common problems are described below.

LR3.5.1 Our Permanence Model.

We mostly behave as though we think everything will or should last forever. Even though in our rational mind we know that it's not true, we cling to it because we are averse to thinking about impermanence. We don't like thinking about old age and death, our own or others. Every time we are reminded of the reality of impermanence, we are disappointed. Perhaps it is better to try and accept impermanence.

LR3.5.2 Our Model of Self

We recognise that we are an individual, one among many. We develop a model of "self ", a sense of who we are. Our vocabulary reflects many uses of the word self, for example, *selfish, self-centred, self-opinionated, self-satisfied, self-less, self-sacrificing, self- esteem, self-respect, self-belief.*

We also use words like *I, me, inner-me, my, myself, inner-self, true-self, mind, soul, spirit, psyche, ego, personality.* They seem to be hard to define, fuzzy concepts. What exactly is self? We feel that our "self" exists and is located somewhere behind our eyes. We can also project an impression of our self out into the world that we perceive around us and imagine *"self"* as the person standing in our shoes. Our model of self may be associated in our mind with what we look like, or with what we can do, or with our values or what we believe in, or how we habitually think and behave. We believe this model to be true. We think of self as an entity, an "it". Its who we are, it's our core being, our soul. We think of this self as existing and being permanent and constant. But we could ask if it's constant, were we born with it? Does it change as we grow up? The way we think and behave depends on how we have been conditioned, so is it our genetic self, or the conditioned one? Our conditioning varies as we go through life, so how can *self* be permanent? If you don't like *yourself* does that mean that there's two of you? (*E.Tolle*) Our view of self may be very different from the one that other's see, based on their own conditioning and beliefs. Which is right?

If we pay too much attention to our model of self, then we become self centred and fail to see how interconnected we are to others and to the world and our role in it. We may also without realising it become too attached to external things that we associate with our model of self, such as treasured possessions or material wealth or concerns about what others think of us. Sometimes it may help us to step out of ourselves and look from a different point of view, see the person standing in our shoes as just a small part of a bigger picture, one of many who share the same needs, and have the same worries.

Sometimes when we observe the behaviour of others it may be helpful to reflect that we do the same things, we have the same vulnerabilities, they are *"just like me "*.

If we fail to grasp that our self is not permanent, then we may not grasp opportunities for positive change, nor notice if we are being negatively influenced.

LR3.5.3 Our Expectations Model

We behave as though we have an *expectation model* of life that we use in certain situations to quickly determine our reaction to events or people in our world. We seem to behave as though this model includes templates or stereotypes or patterns, that we compare with what we perceive, and decide if there is a match. These templates represent how we expect the world to be, how we expect other people to be and how we ourselves should be. We use this model to assess events and evaluate whether what we see matches our expectations. In this way we can quickly evaluate what we perceive as being *good* or *bad*, *acceptable* or *not acceptable*. We then *react* accordingly. This proposed *expectation model* gives us a snap decision, a first impression. We behave as though the expectation model also includes *thresholds* (target levels). These could be thought of as the minimum height of our expectations. We judge something acceptable if it reaches the threshold and unacceptable if it doesn't. Then we react accordingly.

In summary this proposed *expectation model* describes how we use our knowledge and experience to more quickly evaluate and react to situations and people. It helps us stay safe and survive in hostile environments. It also helps us prosper, for example by aiming for high standards in our work.

But this powerful capability that evolution has given us seems to have a downside. It can make us unhappy if we use it continually or inappropriately to make hasty decisions when we don't need to. It can also make us unhappy if we set our expectation threshold of life too high. If we become perfectionists, we set our thresholds at 100 %. It follows that we will perpetually see events and other people and ourselves as less than perfect and therefore as bad and unacceptable. We will perpetually be disappointed and come to feel that life itself is unsatisfactory.

Here is an example. If you were raised by moral parents, you were taught the difference between good and bad, and that any act of crime was a bad thing and was punished. You may have formed an ideal (a model) that good triumphs over bad and all criminals suffer punishment. Later you start to see that in the real world it's not like that. You see people commit serious crimes and " get away with it ". Your ideal doesn't reflect reality, and this can make you feel angry, disappointed, and unhappy. Ideals are good as aims or morals that you choose to live by to make the world a better place. But don't be fooled into thinking that they reflect reality. The world is what it is.

There is another aspect of our expectation model. When we see bad things happen it makes us angry, and we may start to think about what "should" have happened. Then we start to think what we would do if we were in charge and get angry that it's not already happening, because the people in charge seem to us to be incompetent, or stupid or misguided or immoral. But we don't have the authority to implement what we think should happen. We don't control the world. This type of thinking makes us unhappy to no good effect.

If high expectations of life, people, and self are making us unhappy then somehow, we have to learn to change our expectation model of the world. We have to learn that setting high standards and having high expectations is fine in some situations such as work, but it isn't helpful in many other aspects of our personal lives. We have to learn to lower our expectations, accept the world as it is, and other people as they are. We have to learn to accept imperfection and accept that we don't control the world.

LR3.5.4 Failure to See that Everyone's Model of the World is Different.

It was proposed (above) that our mind is conditioned by the sum of our life experience. That includes what we learn in infancy from our parents, from our education, from our work experience, from our peers, family, friends, from our culture, from our religion, from the media and from our direct life experience. This experience is used to create our model of the world, our belief system. It follows that since everyone's life experience is different then so everyone' s models and beliefs are different. The differences can be very great between individuals, between groups and different again across different cultures.

If we cling to our model too strongly, if we don't see that our model is just a model, if we think it's "reality", then we fail to understand the truth that everyone's version of "reality" is different. Given that our model includes our expectations, and levels of acceptability, it follows also that what is acceptable to one person may be totally unacceptable to another. Clinging to our models and beliefs too strongly can lead us to be comfortable only in the company of "like minded" people, and to be averse or intolerant to others. It can cause misunderstandings, can lead us to interact negatively with other people and ultimately can lead to division and strife.

LR3.6 The Work/Life Switch

Evolution equipped us with powerful mental capabilities as we noted above (in LR1 and LR3.1). We can surmise that as hunter gatherers, memory and comparison and prediction helped us to more readily predict where to find food to gather, or how to track animals and how to build shelters. They enabled us to survive. In the present time we learn to refine some of these abilities during our education and training. We apply them at work and may develop them into a very refined set of skills.

Let's take an example, engineering. In this field we analyse the problem to be solved, we need to be very reflective to understand it and gain insight. We also need to be creative to find a solution and analytic to predict the effectiveness of the solution. We plan in great detail the development of the solution and address any potential risks and take steps to avoid them. We learn from previous mistakes. A vital part of the process involves measurement in order to make comparisons in numbers, quality, size and so on. We also are careful to avoid creating hazards, so we check things to be as sure as we can. We can learn to be good at these processes and gain great benefits as a result. We can also get satisfaction and a sense of well-being when we succeed. Similar processes apply to all jobs in varying forms.

If we try and apply these techniques to our personal lives it doesn't seem to work. The very skills that make us successful at work can make us unhappy in our personal lives. The approaches that are very successful in the work may be the exact opposite of what is required in our personal life because the nature of the subjects is so different, they lie in *different dimensions*. These capabilities, which we evolved then further developed, can be very destructive if used in our personal lives inappropriately. Here are some examples:

Measuring to make comparisons is vital in work but can be destructive in your life. It just makes you conscious that some others have more, so you want more, but how many cars can you drive? How much money do you need? How many houses can you live in? (*Comparison is the Thief of Joy. Theodore Roosevelt*)

Analytic thinking and problem solving is crucial at work, but if you try applying it to personal issues that can't be solved that way and you just go round in circles getting stuck in the groove and end up depressed.

The ability to recall past events and learn from them and the ability to plan future outcomes are both powerful at work but if used too much in your personal live you start living in the past or the future. Planning helps us to succeed in many ways especially at work. But the plan isn't reality. If we cling to it as real then, when things don't go to plan, we get disappointed. Sometimes in life it's better to just be more opportunistic.

Assessing the negative aspects of a work project are crucial to pre-empt problems and reduce risk, but if you do this too much in your life you'll get unhappy, and may try to to avoid all risk of failure and so attempt nothing new.

At work we may need to achieve high standards, but perfectionism in our personal lives leads to unhappiness.

At work we strive to continually improve our results. In our personal life we are better to stop the unending quest for more and better.

At work the best managers use words like "us" "we" not "me" and "my" and express their role in terms of *"what they do"* not what their *title* is. But in our personal life, it is not helpful to define ourselves by *"what we do"*.

Interestingly some of these differences in approach to *work* and *life* are embedded in our language. For instance, "careful and careworn " versus "careless and carefree ". They are like two sides of a coin.

Interestingly also, if you look at quotations and sayings, you will find that where most are self-consistent some are contradictory, perhaps because some apply to life and others to work. For example

Failure to plan is planning to fail versus *Don't cross your bridges till you come to them.*

Poor planning leads to poor performance versus. *Live for today, let tomorrow take care of itself.*

If a job is worth doing, it's worth doing well versus *good enough is good enough*

There are many more contradictions like this if you look.

So, it seems that the capabilities that we have evolved, and then refined by education and experience at work, could be the last ones that we need to use in our personal lives. When we finish work, we need to change our mindset, we need to flip the work/ life switch.

LR 4 Learn About Happiness

Introduction

In this root we learn a little about happiness, how it has variously been described, and how it has been measured. We examine some of the many factors that have been found to affect our happiness and some of the various ways we try to find it in our lives. We attempt to integrate these many different aspects of happiness into a new *unified* and *pictorial* model. The model describes how our level of happiness can become high or low, and why. We compare this model with Maslow's Pyramid, with Buddhist ideas on happiness and with psychological ideas on conditioning and we find it broadly compatible. We arrive at a distinction between *external* and *internal* sources of happiness. (This distinction has been reflected in the structure of the Happiness Tree).

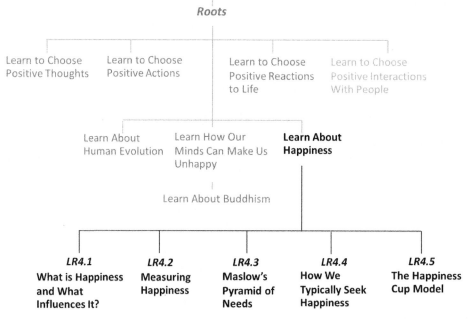

Figure LR4

LR4.1 What is Happiness and What Influences It?

LR4.1.1 What is Happiness?

Happiness is something that everybody wants, but it's intangible, it's a fuzzy concept. We are all different, some of us are more happy than others, and even for one individual, happiness seems to vary with time as circumstances and experiences change. We all have different views on what happiness is and how best to find it.

In order to learn about happiness, we might ask questions such as;

What is happiness?

Is happiness a natural state for humans?

How much is our happiness predetermined by our genes?
How much is it determined by our upbringing and experiences?
How much is it determined by our present lifestyle and circumstances?
How much is it determined by our brain chemistry?
How does our thinking affect our happiness?
What can we do to become happier?
Where can I learn more about it?

In this section we will try to shed light on these questions. We will examine many different views of what happiness is. We will see if it's possible to reconcile them and find a way to show a complete picture.

Many people would agree that happiness is a state of mind. It can range from satisfaction to bliss. We can also experience levels of great unhappiness such as sadness and depression. When we say someone is happy, we don't necessarily mean that they are permanently in a state of joy or bliss, but that they are often in a mental state where they are displaying positive emotions such as satisfaction, contentment, friendliness, and humour, and relatively few negative ones such as sadness, anxiety, anger, hostility and bad humour.

Aristotle, Mencius, Buddha and many others expressed the view that the *quest for lasting happiness is the principal impulse of human activity.* But there are many different opinions as to how to find it. It's not straightforward.

Here's the Wikipedia definition of happiness (en.m.wikipedia.org);
"The term happiness is used in the context of mental or emotional states, including positive or pleasant emotions ranging from contentment to intense joy. It is also used in the context of life satisfaction, subjective well-being, eudaimonia, flourishing and well-being". (Eudaimonia, is a Greek term variously translated as happiness, welfare, flourishing, well-being and blessedness)

Wikipedia also points out that there are many different definitions and gives a wealth of information about the ways in which different philosophical traditions and religions have defined happiness, and the different sources that they considered as leading to happiness. Some of these considered happiness as linked to sensual pleasures, and others to positive experiences in the present moment. Others linked it instead to a reflective sense of well-being or satisfaction with one's lifestyle and success. Still others see happiness as the result of adhering to a moral code. There was considerable debate amongst Greek philosophers about the relative importance of Hedonism versus Eudaimonia (pleasure versus well-being). Nietzsche is one of the few philosophers who *didn't* view happiness as the most important objective, because he felt it prevented us striving for higher goals such as achievement.

Contributors to Wikipedia also had this to say *"Subjective well-being includes measures of current experience (emotions, moods, and feelings) and of life satisfaction. For instance, Sonja Lyubomirsky has described happiness as "the experience of joy, contentment, or positive well-being, combined with a sense that one's life is good, meaningful, and worthwhile.". Xavier Landes has proposed that "happiness includes measures of subjective wellbeing, mood and eudaimonia".*

(It's interesting to note that these definitions do not seem to relate to the *"inner happiness"* sought by the Buddha, nor reflect his teaching that *"cravings"*, for example the pursuit of wealth or pleasure, bring unhappiness).

LR4.1.2 What Influences our Happiness Level?

It's plausible to propose that our Happiness is affected by our Nature (genes), our life conditions/environment, our past and present experiences, our health, our thinking, and our actions.

Our brain chemistry is another factor. Scientists have identified various chemical compounds such as neurotransmitters and hormones that play key roles in our brain function. They affect among other things our mood. These compounds are manufactured by our body. They include *serotonin, catecholamines (dopamine and adrenaline), GABA, endorphins and oxytocin*. They are sometimes called the *feel-good* hormones. If for whatever reason our brain lacks sufficient of these compounds then we can become unhappy, our mood drops. It is known that our lifestyle affects our brain chemistry, for instance exercise boost our endorphins, and hugging a loved one boosts our oxytocin. It's possible that our brain chemistry is also affected by the food we eat (see B6.4). Other factors can lead to a negative effect for example stress, mental exhaustion, and abuse of alcohol or drugs. There are drugs such as SRRIs that can be used to elevate serotonin levels and these are often used to treat depression.

Recently it was proposed that some forms of depression could be caused by inflammation due to infection of the brain (The Inflamed Mind by Prof E Bullmore).

Early researchers concluded that our happiness was *largely fixed*, determined by our genes; we are just born grumpy or happy. More recent research involving identical twins indicated that only about 60% of our happiness is determined by our genes, which is good news because it suggests that we can influence the other 40% by our actions and environment. The experiments aren't precise; the figure could be higher; some studies suggest 50%. (Also our genes may not be such a rigid limitation as previously thought. The new field of *Epigenetics* explores how the actions of our genes can sometimes be modified by our cells in response to our environment and behaviour. Also, our brains are now known to be *plastic*, we can learn to influence our thinking and moods, as we shall see later in UR1).

A movement called *Positive Psychology* emerged according to which our happiness can be thought of as being determined by three factors, our *genes*, our *environment,* and our *actions* (think of these as 3 segments of a Pie Chart). The movement sought to focus on exploring the positive effects that our actions can have on our happiness, rather than focusing (as did many previous studies) on what makes us unhappy. An organisation *Pursuit-of-happiness.org* is exploring the benefits for education that arise from the Positive Psychology and Science of Happiness movements.

LR4.2 Measuring Happiness

Since happiness is so important to us all, it's not surprising that psychologists have sought and found ways of measuring and studying it.

Psychologists Mihaly Csikszentmihaly is regarded as the founder of the *Science of Happiness* movement. He developed *The Experience Sampling Method* whereby subjects periodically recorded their subjective levels of happiness during their daily activities. He applied this method extensively and concluded that we are happier when actively engaged in a task, especially if we are totally engrossed in something challenging and productive *(1990 Flow; the Psychology of Optimal Experience)*.

Martin Seligman *(2002 Authentic Happiness)* and Ed Diener *(The Science of Wellbeing)* continued and extended this theme, making vast numbers of measurements and founding the *Positive Psychology Movement*. Ed Diener (known as *Dr Happiness*) coined the term *Subjective Well Being* (SWB) using categories *"high life satisfaction"*, *"frequent positive feelings"* and *"infrequent negative feelings"*.

Since 2012, a *World Happiness Report* has been published annually by the World Happiness Organisation (WHO). The report is based on worldwide poll of subjective happiness measurements. The results confirm that our happiness is affected by our environment. For example, they show these themes:

- They show a link between freedom and happiness. Some countries that are not democratic get lower scores than democratic countries that are materially poorer.
- The studies show a link between national wealth and happiness, but it is not proportionate. On the one hand it's hard to be happy if you are starving and homeless. On the other hand the wealthiest countries don't necessarily come out top. Relatively poor countries with benign socio-economic-political systems can come high in the league (e.g. Costa Rica)
- Denmark often tops the league. This is usually attributed to its social and political system (good access to housing, education, healthcare, social security), but also strong social and family networks, and also to the fact that many people have hobbies that they pursue together in clubs. It is worth noting that Danish leaders and governments are said to have, for many generations, put the happiness and well-being of the people above national aspirations for military or economic power, and international status.

Increasingly, international philanthropic organisations (*e.g. The Global Happiness Organisation and Action for Happiness*) are influencing governments to take *happiness measurements* into account in addition to economic data such as GDP.

Measurements of a different kind are emerging from the use of MRI brain scanners. Using these, scientists have been able to show that our brains are *plastic* and can be changed by what we do. They have for example measured changes in regions of the brains of subjects who practise meditation. This is consistent with the measurements referred to earlier and reinforces the conclusion that our happiness is determined in part by our actions and not just our genes.

LR4.3 Maslow's Pyramid of Needs

In 1943 a psychologist called Maslow was seeking to explain what motivates or drives human behaviour. He proposed a model of human needs arranged in the form of a pyramid. (The version shown here was drawn from Wikipedia).

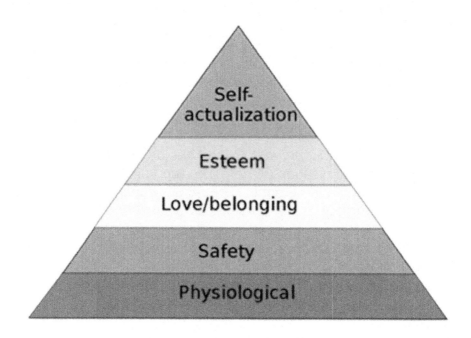

Figure LR4.1 Maslow's Pyramid

- The most *basic physiological* needs for food, water, shelter, warmth, clothing, and rest, are shown at the bottom.
- The next layer up is denoted *safety,* and relates to our need for physical, emotional, and financial security and healthcare.
- The third layer is denoted *love/belonging*, and relates to love, relationships, intimacy, and friends.
- The fourth layer is denoted *esteem,* and relates to being held in esteem, and respected and valued by our peers for our contribution. It also relates to self-esteem, which is influenced by being valued.
- The fifth and top layer denoted *self-actualisation* relates to achievements, such as finding a mate, raising children, using and developing talents, using and developing skills, success at work.

His idea was that the lower levels need to be in place to support the upper ones, and so there is a progression implied. For example, you have to satisfy your basic need for food water and shelter before you can be motivated to pursue the next higher needs. Maslow's model was later criticised by some psychologists because of inaccuracies. He later modified the model to reflect that the levels can actually overlap and also that we can move up or down. The model has nevertheless remained in popular use with sociologists, management trainers, and lifestyle coaches because of its simplicity, and because it's a picture, and because it seems to resonate with our intuition.

Later in life Maslow added another significant level at the top of the pyramid which he called transcendence or *altruism.* This relates to more spiritual needs like helping others, as well as having a benevolent attitude to nature, animals, and the cosmos.

You may notice consistencies between his model and some of the inferences drawn from human evolutionary theory in LR1.

If we try and relate Maslow's Pyramid specifically to happiness, we might infer that progressively moving up the levels increases our happiness. At the lowest level we get pleasure from our food and senses and meeting our basic needs. Then as we progress up the levels, financial, medical, and physical security reduce anxiety and enable us to flourish and move upwards another step. Good relationships make us happy and earning the respect of peers increases our self-esteem. Raising children and achieving career objectives contributes to our happiness and sense of well-being.

You might infer that it is hard to be happy if you can't meet the lowest levels, for example if you are starving, homeless and trapped in a war zone, then you can't move up to gain the happiness of the higher levels.

The type of economic/political/social conditions of the country that we live in affects our happiness as does our degree of freedom. Maybe, in Maslow's model this can be viewed as affecting the ease with which we can move between the levels and have the freedom to do so.

LR4.4 How We Typically Seek Happiness

Most people would say that above all they want to be happy, though it's not obvious how to achieve it. We can't analyse our way to a solution, and we don't learn about it at school. But we do know that we must meet our human needs by working to earn a living, to pay for food and shelter, and to achieve a measure of financial and physical security, as well as medical care and education, so we get on with that.

We seek happiness in sensual pleasures like food, drink, sex and in aesthetic pleasure. We also find pleasure through various forms of entertainment and leisure pursuits.

We try to avoid things that we are averse to, or to delay them.

We learn that, for many of us, isolation can make us unhappy, and that good relationships make us happy.

We learn that poverty, lack of food and shelter, and ill health and many of life's problems can make us unhappy.

We learn that success can bring many benefits including a sense of achievement, esteem, and material wealth.

We learn that wealth gives status, security, access to many pleasures, good healthcare, and the power to get rid of many of our problems.

So, although we want above all else to be happy, because we don't know how to, we may defer it till later. We may tend to work hard now to be successful, and therefore wealthier later. We think that after we've succeeded in life, then happiness will naturally follow. Or we may think that we will have more leisure time to search for happiness later on, after we've succeeded. In this way we see happiness as a *destination* that we will get to later.

But real life doesn't seem to work like that. We see people who have worked hard to achieve vast wealth and fame but remain unhappy and still strive for more. We see some who remain unhappy even when they have everything, and others who are happy even though they have almost nothing. It seems that, once you've got enough to live on, you can't find happiness by striving for more, that just postpones happiness.

We find that endless pleasure and endless leisure time don't make us happy for long. We get bored.

Problems such as ill health or extreme poverty make us unhappy, but the converse isn't true. A lack of all material or health problems doesn't make us happy.

We find putting things off that we are averse to actually makes us unhappier because we magnify the perceived difficulty of doing them, whereas if we get on and do them, we feel happier.

So we learn that some things in our lives make us happier but more of them doesn't make us any happier, and sometimes the happiness doesn't last. We learn that some things make us unhappy, but their absence doesn't make us happy. And doing some things we don't want to do makes us happier. It's very confusing, no wonder we struggle to be happy, we struggle even to express it in words. It may help to visualise happiness, by an analogy described below.

LR4.5 The Happiness Cup Model

Imagine that you have a cup that represents your mind. Your happiness flows into this cup from various sources, which you can think of as taps above your cup. If some of the taps are turned on, and your cup doesn't leak, then it will fill up and overflow with happiness. This can happen even if the taps are only half on and the flow is small. It can also happen with some of the taps turned off. See Figure LR4.2

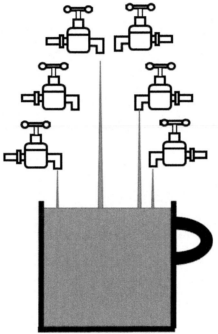

Figure LR4.2

Each tap represents a source of happiness, for example:
- enjoying life's pleasures.
- having fun.
- job satisfaction.
- satisfaction with your ability to provide for your family's needs (food, shelter etc).
- positive relationships, intimacy, and raising children.
- earning respect.
- learning something new.
- achievement, success.
- helping others.

You could choose to order the taps in a sequence that matches Maslow's pyramid, (for example putting *achievement* and *helping others* at the top).

Turning on the taps relates to growing a happier healthier lifestyle. But some of these taps (eg pleasure) contribute to your happiness but don't stay turned on for so long, so they alone may not fill your cup, and some can even be corrosive and make holes in your cup (overeating, addiction, overworking).

If your cup has holes in the bottom, then, even with all the taps turned fully on it will not fill, the level of your happiness will stay low. See Figure LR4.3

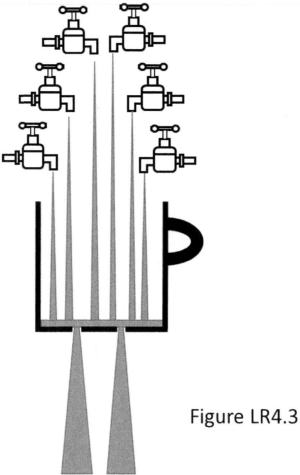

Figure LR4.3

The holes in the cup represent any negative conditioning of your mind. They can include, for example, negative thinking, regrets of the past, worrying about the future, unrealistic expectations, perfectionism, greed, envy, intolerance, hatred, meanness, low self-esteem, and failure to accept the way things are. Some forms of mental illness might relate to particular types of holes in the cup.

If you lack the basics of food, shelter, security, and company, then it's harder to be happy because you lack the capability to reach the taps to turn them on. In addition, the worry and insecurity you experience may create holes in your cup.

Similarly, if you are physically ill, then you may lack the capability to reach the taps to turn them on, and the incapacity and pain you experience may create holes in your cup.

This model draws a distinction between the *external* sources of happiness, the taps (located in the branches of your lifestyle) and the *inner* causes of unhappiness, the holes (which are addressed in the roots)

This model seems to be consistent with the observations we previously noted:

- It is possible to be rich and successful and yet be unhappy (all the taps fully on but there's some holes in the cup).
- It's possible to be materially poor and yet be happy (some taps half on but no holes).
- It might explain why some successful people strive to acquire still more wealth, because it's the process of achieving that makes them happy, not just the wealth.
- It explains why aversion and procrastination affect our happiness. Because we worry about having to confront things we are averse to or carry out tasks that don't want to do, then this makes a hole in our cup. If we instead confront them or get on with the task we get a sense of achievement, so we fix a hole and turn on a tap.
- If we choose to defer happiness and treat it as a destination, then that corresponds to striving to turn on all the taps but not fixing the holes. If we treat happiness as a journey, then that corresponds to fixing the holes whilst turning on some of the taps.
- It might explain why children tend to be happier than adults. Their basic needs are provided for by their parents (the tap has been turned on by the parents). Their minds have not yet been conditioned negatively so there are no holes in the cup. They have love from parents and family, have boundless curiosity and everything is new, so they are learning continually. They play at every opportunity. With all these taps on and no holes in the cup they are happy (although the levels appear to vary between individuals).

The Happiness Cup model seems to be able to accommodate a wide range of different views and ideas of happiness in one model, for example:

It seems to be able to accommodate the differing *definitions* of happiness that we examined earlier (even Nietzsche's view). It includes taps that relate to pleasure seeking, but also those that relate to a sense of wellbeing from succeeding in life and earning respect and from a sense of achievement.

The Cup analogy is broadly compatible with Maslow's pyramid. If you can't satisfy your basic needs for food and shelter, you cannot reach even the lowest tap to turn it on, so your cup stays empty. As you move up the pyramid you are more able to reach and turn on the higher taps (such as achievement), and so increase the number of your sources of happiness. Your ability to move up the levels and turn on more taps is influenced by your socio-economic environment.

The Cup model seems compatible with the Positive Psychology themes that our happiness is affected by our environment, our genes and our actions, but adds an important fourth factor; our ***thoughts*** affect our happiness.

We can also relate this Cup model to the Buddhas teaching. The mindless pursuit of pleasure can make us unhappy (turns on a tap but corrodes a hole in our cup). Craving material wealth can also be viewed as turning on a tap but creates negative mental states that create holes in the bottom. Finding and fixing the holes in the cup relates to the Buddhist concept of cultivating our minds, eliminating negative traits. If we can do this, we generate inner happiness, we can remain happy even with the taps turned down.

We can relate fixing the holes in the cup with aspects of *psychotherapy*. We can relate some different forms of unhappiness such as *anhedonia* with an inability to turn on the pleasure taps (it's as though they've seized up).

The purpose of the Happiness Tree model is to help you to both find and fix the holes in your cup and turn on the taps.

It is ironic that given the importance we all attach to happiness, it's a subject that is not normally part of our education. We don't learn about it at school or even in adult education. Aristotle had this to say *"Educating the mind without educating the heart is no education at all"*

Part 3. The Upper Roots: Cultivating Your Mind.

Introduction

The Upper Roots deal with the process of learning to *Cultivate Your Mind* to generate *Inner Happiness.* Information has been drawn from the Lower Roots and other sources. The author has taken the liberty of interpreting that information and then re-presenting it in a particular structured way that is aimed at making it easier to understand, learn, and remember.

We have discussed in *LR2* and *LR3* that (along with our genes) our *conditioned* mind greatly influences everything that we think, everything that we do, how we react to life and how we interact with people. Our thoughts, actions, reactions, and interactions can be positive or negative, and they determine how happy we feel The information in this section is about learning to cultivate or re-condition our minds so that we choose to think and behave in ways that generate more positive outcomes, enabling us to find *inner happiness* and develop. *mental resilience.* Interwoven in these roots are the themes of *virtue* and *compassion* which also help to make our world happier.

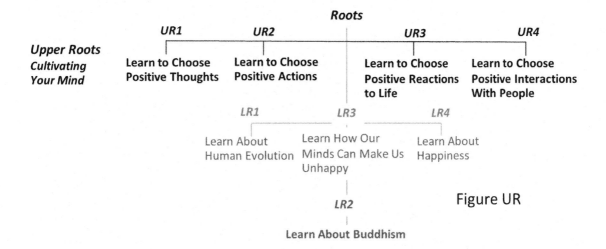

UR1 Learn to Choose Positive Thoughts

Introduction.

We proposed in *LR2* and *LR3* that it is our thoughts (rather than events) that determine how we feel, and that negative thoughts make us unhappy. We also proposed that when our mind is not focused on any purposeful activity, then, it becomes host to a stream of uninvited thoughts (the monkey mind, the untamed mind) that tend to be negative. One obvious way to reduce our negative thinking is to improve our lifestyle in a way that keeps our mind more engaged in purposeful activity (work, play, socialising etc.) for more of the time. However, we may not always be able to do this, there may be times when we are alone and vulnerable to negative thinking. In this section we present some techniques (derived from Buddhism and Mindfulness) that help us solve this problem, such that we have fewer negative thoughts and more positive ones. These are shown in Figure UR1 below.

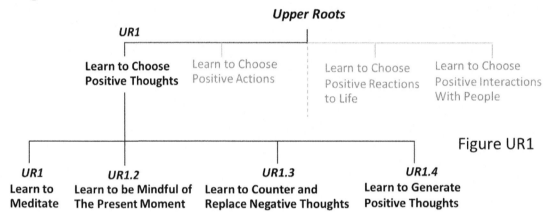

Figure UR1

UR1.1 Learn to Meditate

Introduction

In this subsection we will learn about some specific meditation techniques and the powerful positive effects that they can have on our thinking and happiness.

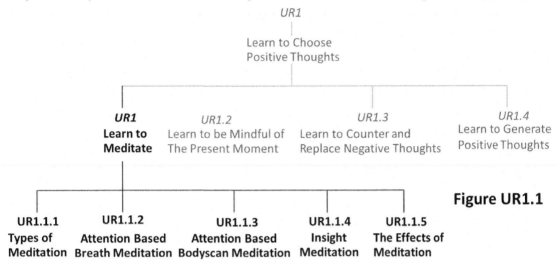

Figure UR1.1

UR1.1.1 Types of Meditation.

The word meditation is derived from the latin *meditatum*, meaning to *ponder*. Meditation has been practised in various forms for thousands of years in different cultures and religions, with varied spiritual, religious, or training objectives. There are many different forms of meditation techniques. For example, you may come across terms like transcendental meditation, visualization meditation, mantra meditation, spiritual meditation, mindfulness meditation, and focused meditation. There's also attention-based meditation, insight meditation, loving kindness meditation, gratitude meditation, progressive relaxation meditation, movement meditation and guided meditation. Both Yoga and Qi Gong involve elements of meditation. Prayer and music are considered by some as forms of meditation. The boundaries between these different forms of meditation are a bit fuzzy, though they share some underlying features.

Here we will talk about a specific form of *attention-based meditation,* in which the mind is focused on the *breath*. It is also referred to as *single point of focus meditation,* and *breath meditation*. It is the form of meditation taught by the Bhudda to train concentration and awareness, and to achieve a mentally clear and calm state of mind. (it corresponds to *Right Concentration / Jhana / Samatha / Calmness*). We will also learn about another form of attention-based meditation called the *bodyscan,* which has come from the Mindfulness tradition, in which attention is focused on the various internal body sensors in sequence.

We will also touch on, but not fully explore, *Insight Meditation*, which is the second form taught by the Buddha and aims to give us greater insight into the human condition and to see more clearly the way things are (this corresponds to *Right* Concentration / Jhana / Vipassana).

The Happiness Tree

UR1.1.2 Attention-Based Breath Meditation.

What Is Attention-Based Breath Meditation?

It is a training exercise aimed at calming and cultivating the mind, and so increasing our sense of well-being.

What It Isn't:

- It isn't mystical, or exotic, or an escape from reality.
- It's not about going into a trance, or having strange experiences, (though you may experience some).
- It's not a form of relaxation exercise, though you may become relaxed.
- It's not a form of deep thinking or problem solving.
- It's not self-centered, though it appears to be so at first. Gradually it changes our view of the world.
- It isn't about trying to have no thoughts, but about focusing attention and becoming aware when you are distracted by thoughts.

How to Start

Select a place where you won't be disturbed, and which is reasonably quiet and peaceful. It helps if it's a pleasant setting that you're comfortable with. To start with always use the same place. Later, when you've had more experience, the setting is less critical, you can do it anywhere. It's useful to have a timer that you can set to tell you when you have completed a session.

Sit in an upright chair, but don't rest your back on the chair, keep your back upright. This stops your body getting too relaxed. Keep your feet flat on the floor, your hands in your lap palms up. Tilt your chin down slightly without lolling your head forwards.

Calm your mind for a few minutes, reflect on the benefits of meditation and the method that you are going to use, then close your eyes and focus your attention on your body.

Breathe in and out deeply and strongly, repeat this several times.

Focus on any sounds or smells that you can sense around you and be aware of them for a few minutes, just attending to your senses.

Now switch your attention to your breath. Feel the sensations as it moves in and out through your nostrils and feel your diaphragm move up and down. Now focus your attention entirely on the sensations in your nostrils as your breath moves in and out. Notice that the air you breathe in is cooler than the air you breathe out. Continue breathing and maintaining this concentrated attention for as long as you can, feeling each breath pass in and out of your nostrils.

At some point, no matter how hard you try, uninvited thoughts will arise in your mind and distract your attention away from your breath. When you become aware of this simply draw your attention back to your breath. Don't regard the distraction as failure, it's normal and part of the training process. Each time you are distracted simply become aware of it and bring your attention back to the breath. Keep doing this repeatedly till you reach the end of the session (which could typically last from 10 to 45 minutes).

This is at first a strange and difficult practice. The most important thing is not how "well" you do but whether you're prepared to keep on doing it, trusting that the investment will pay you back.

If you meditate regularly then after a while you may start to notice things about how the mind works. You may for example notice that some thoughts are fleeting, and you can quickly detach from them. Others temporarily take over the mind, you get lost in a train of thought that can jump from one topic to another many times and last several minutes. You may experience a different kind of thought that is fleeting and not rational and which passes before you can remember it. This kind of thought is more like a dream, and you may be close to falling asleep.

To begin with you will probably not like to meditate, it may seem pointless and boring. So, it's very easy to skip it, and get on instead with more interesting or demanding tasks in your busy schedule. But if you persist, then after a while you may start to notice a feeling of calmness after a session. You may come to value this calmness that each session brings, and so be more willing to make the effort.

When should I Meditate?
The benefits are cumulative, you need to meditate often, ideally say 10 to 45 minutes every day. Because of this most people choose a set time and build it into their routine so they're less likely to skip it. You will find that if you have been busy thinking about some problem or other before meditating, then your mind may generate a stream of thoughts relating to what you were previously thinking about. Maybe this is one reason why many people choose to meditate early in the morning before work, but it's not a fixed rule. Some like to meditate in the afternoon, as a refresher, and others in the evening, as a means of calming down prior to sleep.

What is the Best Way to Learn to Meditate?
Ideally, if you want to make rapid progress, and you are fortunate enough, the best way is to find an experienced teacher, or enroll on a course, or go on a retreat. Alternatively use some of the many resources now available (there are many books, web sites, audio cd's and video's, on-line courses, meditation phone apps, and YouTube videos). You could also join a local group. But remember meditation requires no special equipment and so if these options aren't open to you, just get on and do it yourself.

Some Tips on Meditation
You don't need to understand how or why meditation works. You just need to trust it enough to try it for a while. If you do this, you will experience the benefits for yourself and no longer need to take it on trust. Bear in mind that:
- It isn't easy, or quick, it needs concentration and perseverance.
- It's not a success or fail activity, you just have to keep doing it.
- It doesn't matter how often you get distracted, there's no scoring.
- You could say the only measure of success in meditation is continuing to do it every day.

When your mind wanders you may feel angry and frustrated. Think instead that the more it wanders the more opportunities you are getting to practice being aware and bringing your attention back to your breath.

You may be meditating one day and find that your mind is unusually agitated. Remind yourself that the mind varies from day to day, minute to minute. Sometimes it is more calm and sometimes more agitated, that's normal. Don't give up, just keep repeatedly bringing your attention back to the breath, treat it as a learning opportunity to be exploited.

The most important thing about meditating is to do it every day. It is said that the greatest obstacle to meditation is just failing to do it **regularly**.

As a beginner you may find meditation difficult, and boring, and find reasons to stop doing it. Therefore, it's a good idea to think about how to build it into your daily routine, and how to motivate yourself to persevere, so that you don't get lazy and skip it. Some ways to do this are:

- Start with a short meditation, say 5 or 10 minutes, but rigidly adhere to it at the same time every day, then gradually increase the time.
- Anchor it to something else that's already in your routine (eg before your morning cup of tea, or after you clean your teeth or before you go to work).
- When you skip a session ask yourself why, then try to remove the problem that caused it.
- Continually remind yourself of the benefits and why you are doing it.
- Keep a tally of how many days in a row you manage before missing a session and see if you can beat your own record.

As you get experienced you will value the time spent meditating and happily devote more time to it.

Variations on Attention Based Meditation

It is said that there are as many variations as there are meditators.

- You may be flexible enough to use the traditional lotus position in which you sit cross legged on the floor.
- You can try meditating lying down (but you may fall asleep).
- If you have difficulty focusing on or sensing the breath in your nostrils you can experiment with breathing more deeply, or more forcefully, or more slowly. Try and detect in your nostril the *coolness* of the in breath and the *warmth* of the out breath.
- You can as an alternative focus on your breathing through sensing the rise and fall of your abdomen.
- You can use the alarm timer on your phone to let you know when your set time is up. Alternatively use a meditation app such as *Insight Timer*, or simply use a clockwork kitchen timer wrapped in a towel to muffle it a little.
- Initially try silently counting your breathing cycles. Counting can be a useful prop when learning to meditate because it may help you avoid being distracted too easily. It is usually recommended not to count above 10.
- An example of a counting method is to count 10 sets of 10 breathing cycle repetitions. So, near the end of the first in breath you silently count 1, then

at the end of the first out breath you count 1, at the end of the second in breath you count 2 , at the end of the second out breath you count 1 (because it's still the first set). The counting sequence will thus be 1.1, 2.1 etc. to10.1, then 1.2, 2.2 etc to 10.2 and so on, till after 100 breaths you reach 10.10). You'll find that if your breathing cycle is normally 6 seconds, then 10 sets of 10 breaths takes roughly 10 minutes.

- You can use this as a way of defining the length of a session, for example 10 sets of 10 makes a good target for a beginner, then progress to say 3 sets of 10 repetitions which will take about 30 minutes (depending on how fast you breathe).
- You could count a different way using letters and numbers, 1a,2a....10a, 1b,2b...10j.
- Some people count the number of breaths until distracted by a thought then reset the counter to zero.
- Counting is useful, but you must be careful not to be distracted by the numbers or you may lose the focus on your breath. For that reason, it's better to focus only on the breath at the start of each in and out breath and delay counting the number till just before you near the end of the in or out breath.
- Some experts advocate not counting once you have become more experienced.
- Some meditators count how long it takes to breathe in and out and regulate the speed of their breathing for example, 4 counts in, 4 counts out.
- You may find, if you breathe slowly that you can sense your heartbeat, and you could count say 4 heartbeats per breath.
- Others repeat a mantra relating to the breath, like "in" and "out", or "om" or, "not thinking".

As you become more experienced in meditation, you may be able to meditate almost anywhere, and any time. You may be able to make use of enforced idle time such as queuing, waiting for a bus or travelling, or when doing something boring. You can also meditate when at any time when you are overwhelmed with persistent thoughts, or when you can't get to sleep.

You can try walking meditation. Do this in a clear space with an even surface. Keep your eyes open and your head looking downwards. You walk slowly and synchronise one breath with one step. As you walk you pay attention to your breath and to the sensations in your feet, noting the changes in pressure in your heels, soles and toes as you shift weight from one foot to the other.

UR1.1.3 Attention-Based Bodyscan Meditation

This form of meditation was introduced by Jon Kabat-Zinn as part of his MBSR stress reduction initiative. To learn this exercise it is helpful to be talked through it as you do it. You will find *guided meditation* videos on YouTube by Jon Kabat-Zinn and others.

Find a quiet comfortable place where you won't be disturbed for the 20 or so minutes needed for this exercise. Wear comfortable, loose-fitting clothes. Lie down on your back on the floor or on a bed with a firm but comfortable mat or mattress underneath you and a pillow under your head. Place your hands by your side and your feet hip width apart (this is the Yoga *Corpse* pose). The exercise begins with a relaxation stage. Feel your breath going in and out and let yourself sink into the mat. Next focus on your feet, and as you breath out relax any tension you can feel there. Then focus on your legs and as you breath out relax any tension you can feel in your leg muscles. Continue this muscle relaxing process on your arms and hands, abdomen, chest, shoulders neck and head, to relax your whole body.

Now you are ready to start the body scan. You are going to slowly scan down your whole body from the top of your head to the tips of your toes, paying attention to any sensations you feel in each area as it is scanned (think of a spotlight moving slowly down your body).

You have many *inner* sensors distributed throughout your body, constantly sending messages to your brain. The sensations you feel might arise from sensors in your skin, your scalp, your nerves, muscles, joints and inner organs. The sensations might include warmth or coolness, tension or lightness, pain or discomfort, contact pressure, pulsing, movement, sensitivity, numbness. tingling, itching, or moving air. You may feel no sensation in some areas, be aware of this as well.

Start with your scalp, focus on any sensations you can detect there. Notice the nature of the sensations, accept them without judging them as good or bad, then move onto the forehead and temples and note any sensations you can detect there.

Continue this process scanning in turn your eyes, nose, cheeks, mouth. Then scan your chin, jaw and ears. Then the back of your head, and the top of your neck and down to your shoulders. Move down to your upper arms, forearms, wrists, and hands. Then move to your chest, ribs, upper back and shoulder blades. When your attention wanders just bring it back to your body sensations.

Continue moving the spotlight down your spine and lower back, and abdomen, notice the movement due to your breath, and any sensation from your inner organs. Then progress down through your hips and groin, your thighs, knees, shins, calves, to your feet and toes.

Finally bring the scan to an end by feeling your whole body, relaxed and present in the moment.

Like the breath meditation, the bodyscan exercise helps train attention, concentration, and an awareness of when your mind has wandered. In addition, it develops an increasing awareness of your body, something that we often lack. It is very relaxing and may send you to sleep.

UR1.1.4 Insight Meditation
What Is It?
Experienced meditators, once they have learned to calm the mind using the breath, move on to learn a more advanced form called Insight Meditation (Vipassana, seeing things clearly) This form of meditation was taught by the Buddha as a way of gaining beneficial insight into the way the mind works, and to see more clearly the true nature of things. He taught that it was a way to clear the mind by letting go of material cravings and negative traits, and to see that some of our models of the world are false. This more advanced form of meditation is beyond the scope of this book and may need to be taught by an instructor. You can find more information online. It seems to be practised in different ways according to which source you consult. We present below a very brief overview.
How Is It Done?

Begin with attention-based breath meditation. Then, having calmed and cleared your mind, move your attention away from the breath and focus attention on a particular theme regarding the human condition and the nature of things. The themes emphasised by the Buddha, were *Impermanence*, *Suffering* (the unsatisfactory nature of life), and the concept of *Self*. Because your mind was cleared of clutter by the breath meditation you may be more able to see things more clearly. You may gain beneficial insight into the way that your mind works and the way that it has been conditioned.

You can choose to reflect on other themes. For example, negative traits and how we can detach from them; coping with grief or pain; how to be more compassionate, or less angry, or how to reduce hatred.

Some sources describe Insight Meditation in a different way. They describe the process as concentrating on the physical sensations of the breath through the rising and falling of the abdomen whilst noting thoughts that come and go, and categorising them without dwelling on them, using generalized labels such as *thinking, remembering, planning, visualizing*, and being aware of any external interruptions without dwelling on them.

UR1.1.4 The Effects of Meditation
What are the claimed benefits of meditation?
During each session we become relaxed. We also spend more time in the present moment, which gives us a temporary respite from negative thinking (*monkey mind*). In the opinion of experienced meditators, this practice makes us calmer and happier, as well as developing increased concentration and heightened awareness of the sensations in our body. Having reduced the clutter in our minds and calmed it, we may also be able to see things more clearly.

The Buddha believed that meditation also helps in the development of other valued human qualities, for example making us less greedy, more compassionate, more tolerant, more accepting, and more able to see the true nature of things. (It therefore helps us to develop the positive qualities discussed subsequently in the other upper roots UR2, UR3, UR4).

He also believed that meditation makes us less focused on *self* and gives us more a feeling of *dual-awareness* or *oneness* with the world. Advanced meditators are indeed able to experience this state of unity with the world where the boundaries of self and the environment dissolve. They are more focused on events in the present moment and less prone to mind wandering.

How does meditation work?

We don't know how meditation works. It could be that the repeated practice develops our powers of *concentration* (on the breath) and our *awareness* (of distracting thoughts), and that this repetition somehow changes our (plastic) mind, perhaps by changing the default settings or connections. Or maybe it's the increased time spent in the present moment that brings the benefits? Or maybe it's the time spent in a calmed state of mind where our brain waves are in the lower alpha and theta frequencies? Or maybe it's the insights that we gain with a calmed mind? Or maybe it's a combination of these things?

What evidence is there that meditation works?

Monk meditators report extreme happiness, despite living in austerity. This has been reported by meditators over a period of two and a half thousand years.

Experienced meditators in present times report increased happiness, calmness, and equanimity.

There are documented reports (MBSR) of the benefits of *"mindfulness"* techniques in psychotherapy such as reduced stress and anxiety..

There is medical evidence that meditation and mindfulness practices can produce positive, measurable physical changes in our bodies, for example reducing markers of stress.

It would be incorrect to say that there is a complete scientific consensus that meditation works, but it is a field of intense research and there is already considerable evidence rolling in. Some of the earliest studies used Electroencephalography (EECG) whereby electrodes are placed on the skull to measure brainwaves (electrical activity in the brain). These studies showed that during meditation the frequency and amplitude of the waves in particular regions decreased, supporting the view that meditation induces *calmness*. More recently MRI brain scans have shown in several studies that the brain is plastic and can be positively altered by long term meditation. Areas associated with negative aspects such as anxiety become smaller, and areas associated with positive aspects such as cognitive function and problem solving, become bigger. In consequence some of our personal qualities, are no longer to be thought of as fixed, but as changeable by training; (note how this matches Buddha's description of "cultivating the mind").

Positive *reports* in the media are now commonplace. For example, an article in Forbes.com, 9 Feb 2015 listed *seven ways that meditation can change the brain*. These included helping to preserve the aging brain, reduced activity in the DMN (the Default Mind Network or monkey mind network), anti-depressant anti-anxiety and stress reduction effects. It also cites decreases in the volume of the amygdala (the part of the brain associated with fear anxiety and stress), increases in volume of the hippocampus (associated with learning and memory) and in areas associated with emotional regulation and self-referential processing. Other improvements included, increased concentration and attention, and reduced addiction. Some changes are said to have been noted after only 8 weeks of practice.

Another Forbes article, 20 Oct 2022 by Zamena Mejia, lists *10 science backed benefits of meditation* as stress reduction, anxiety management, depression management, lower blood pressure, stronger immune system, improved memory, improved mood regulation and increased self-awareness.

A recent article in BigThink.com Oct 25 2022 by Mobelo Costandi described how scientists have shown that meditation changes the brain's topography. It alters the interconnections between different regions in the brain and inverts the normal priority in such a way that the DMN (monkey mind network) takes lower priority than the Central Executive Network CEN (involved in attention to our external and internal sensors). Advanced meditators display more activity in the CEN than the DMN especially in the dorsolateral prefrontal cortex (dlPFC). This may explain why advanced meditators experience the feeling of *oneness* with the world described previously.

There are also reports of negative side effects in a minority of people whose symptoms were made worse by meditation, though this has not been extensively researched. For example someone who is suffering from depression might already be too focused inwards, and might benefit more from externally focused activities like outdoor exercise.

UR1.2 Choose to be Mindful of the Present Moment.

UR1.2.1 The Problems of Living in the Past or Future
In *LR3* and *LR4*, we described that when our mind is focused on some purposeful activity (for example, work, play, conversation or solving a problem) it is *engaged*. We tend to be happier in this state.

We also learned that our mind, if not purposefully engaged, wanders *(the monkey mind)*, and often starts to think about the past and the future. It generates negative thoughts based on regrets of past actions and worries about the future. These are some of the most frequent and most toxic negative thoughts that we have, they give rise to unhappiness, stress and anxiety and so are worthy of special attention.

In section *LR1* we suggested that our hunter gatherer ancestors probably lived entirely *in the moment* with little thought for the past or future. By contrast in the modern world many of us spend a large portion of our day worrying about the past and the future. Evolution did not equip us to deal with this situation, which may be why it can become such a serious problem.

If you kept a log of how much time you spent ruminating, thinking about the past or the future you might get a nasty surprise. It might persuade you that you need instead to find ways to live more in the present.

An obvious step is to make changes to your lifestyle, scheduling more activities and social events as part of your routine so that your mind is more often engaged and has less time for rumination. We address this in UR2 and in the *branches*.

The attention-based meditations previously described in UR1.1 also help because they anchor the meditator to the present moment. Yoga, Chi Gong, Tai Chi and other *mind-body* practices also keep the participant in the moment.

However, there will still be times when you are not fully engaged (e.g. waiting for a bus on your own), and when doing something that you can do automatically (e.g. walking). At such times you remain vulnerable to negative thinking. In this section we explore this problem further and examine some techniques to help us deal with it.

UR1.2.2 The Importance of Now

An important first step is to realise and accept that the *present* is all that we have, and our *senses* are the only way of experiencing it.

The *past* does not exist, except in our memories and in the minds of others (and each of us has a different view of it).

Because the past doesn't exist, we can't change it. We can learn from our experiences and move on, we can have pleasant memories, but continued regrets don't help us.

The *future* doesn't exist except in our imagination and our plans. We know that our actions have consequences that we experience later, so it is reasonable to have some broad plan. But once we've got a plan we should return to the present, knowing that whatever eventually happens, we will deal with at that time.

UR1.2.3 Being Mindful of the Present Moment

The ability to focus our awareness on the present moment is often referred to as *Mindfulness*, but also sometimes as *Prescence*. It corresponds to the Buddhist view of *Right Mindfulness*. which involves *keeping in mind and maintaining an awareness of the present sensations of the body, the nature of the experience (pleasant, unpleasant, or neutral), the state of one's mind, and mental phenomena as they arise, without reference to their meaning in the context of the outside world* (i.e., without comparing, assessing or judging).

The most widely used definition of mindfulness is the "operational" one proposed by Jon Kabat-Zinn; *"mindfulness is the awareness that arises from paying attention, on purpose, in the moment, non-judgmentally"*.

When our mind is fully *engaged* it is often processing data from the outside world in real time and deciding how to react. We are in this state most of the time when working or playing or engaged in conversation.

However, if our mind finds the scenario it is engaged with to be of insufficient interest, then it stops paying full attention. It *disengages* and switches to *default* mode, which allows it to wander into the imaginary world. For example, this is more likely to happen if we sense no threat or prospect of reward, or if we see nothing exciting or unusual to maintain our attention. However, if we deliberately, mindfully, choose to pay full attention to all the sensations that we are experiencing, **even though we don't need to**, then we may create enough interest, or pleasure, or notice new things, sufficient to delay our mind switching to default mode and producing negative thoughts. If we can learn to do this often in our everyday lives then we become less vulnerable to negative thinking. We may also learn to fully enjoy the present rather than rushing on to the next activity.

UR1.2.4 Mindfulness Exercises

There are many *Mindfulness Exercises* that can be used, to help us learn to become more mindful of the present. A few examples are given here.

1 *Take Your Time, Smell the Roses.*

When you engage in any pleasurable or uplifting activities, make sure that you don't rush through them; slow down. Take time to fully savour the sensations and become fully aware of the various elements that you experience. Notice the positive feelings that they generate but choose to detach from comparing, assessing, or judging. Focus your attention on everything that you experience, the sights, sounds, tastes, smells and feel of everything around you.

2 *Eating Mindfully*

Choose some small object to eat, like a raisin or grape or an apple or orange. Think about where it came from, how it was grown, who grew it, and how it came to you. Focus your whole attention on it. Notice everything that you can from your senses. Notice the appearance, take in every detail. Notice the feel and texture of the skin. Notice the smell. Notice when you start to eat it, the texture, and how it feels in your mouth. Notice the taste. Eat it deliberately slowly. Extract the maximum sensation and pleasure from your eating, be conscious of it. Apply the same approach when you eat a meal, take time, pay attention to it, be in the present rather than rushing to get onto the next activity.

3 *Walking Mindfully*

When you go for a walk, make a conscious effort to be aware of what your senses are telling you as you progress. Notice what you can see, focus your eyes on specific objects, note, the shapes, the colours, the movement. Notice for example the trees and vegetation, the sky, the pathway, any animals, or other people. Notice what you can hear, for example the sound of wind in the trees, the sound of birds or other animals, any noise of traffic. Notice what you can feel, for example the sun or wind or rain on your face, the feel of the ground under your feet.

UR1.3 Learn to Counter and Replace Negative Thoughts

UR1.3.1 Learn to Recognise and Categorise Your Thoughts

Make the effort to become more aware of your thoughts. Try to recognise and categorise them as *positive, negative, neutral* or *untimely*. Notice how they make you feel.

- *Positive thoughts* make you feel good.
- *Negative thoughts* tend to make you feel bad and are the main cause of unhappiness.

- *Neutral* thoughts are those which are inconsequential. An example is a mental *narrative* in which you are thinking about something that you wish you could say to someone, even though you're not ever going to be able to. Neutral thoughts may not *directly* make you unhappy, but they occupy mind space, distract you from doing something more useful or enjoyable, drain your energy and serve no useful purpose.(Having said that mental narratives can be positive and useful as a way of rehearsing or planning for future events. Also, when we are musing, a neutral thought can sometimes link or lead us to a positive one by suggesting a new approach or creative solution).
- *Untimely* thoughts. Some thoughts may be positive but untimely. For example, thoughts on a solution to a work-related problem may be positive, but if they keep coming at the wrong time (e.g., during leisure time, or when you need to sleep) then they can have negative impact. They can make you exhausted and unhappy.

UR1.3.2 Learn How to Treat Your Thoughts.

When you recognise a timely positive thought welcome it as a guest, reward it with your attention, feed it so it is more likely to come back, develop it to create other positive thoughts.

When you recognise a negative thought, treat it like an unwelcome guest, detach from it, don't reward it with attention, it is then less likely to return.

When you recognise a neutral thought, decide if it's worth the attention you're giving it and if its not helpul or leading in a positive direction detach from it.

When you recognize a positive but untimely thought, welcome it, promise yourself that you will deal with it later, (maybe write a reminder), then forget it.

UR1.3.3 Learn to Classify Your Negative Thoughts

Take the time to classify the types of negative thought you have and notice which ones come most often. Everyone's list will be different but there are some common themes. You might notice categories such as regrets about the past, worries about the future, worried by events in the news, thoughts of dissatisfaction with aspects of your life, or yourself or others. You may notice thoughts arising from toxic traits such as greed, envy, jealousy, hatred etc. You may find that some types of negative thought arise from habits such as comparing what you have with others.

UR1.3.4 Learn to Analyse Persistent Negative Thoughts

Persistent negative thoughts are particularly toxic. If we experience them over and over again, we can get stuck in the groove and become obsessed with them. This can lead to depression. It can be helpful to analyse the cause of such a persistent thought. We can try to understand what is behind it and what triggers it, then find ways to avoid the trigger. It can also be helpful to test if the thought is actually based on reason or is it irrational or wildly exaggerated? Rationalising in this way can help us disarm a thought by realising it to be untrue and having no basis in reality.

UR1.3.5 Replace the Negative thought With A Positive One

Having analysed a negative thought, deliberately look for positive counter thoughts. Here are some examples to show what is meant; -

If you're worried about some possible future event, you might instead remind yourself that you have already prepared a plan to deal with the future eventualities, that you can do nothing more about it at present, and that you're not achieving anything more by continuing to worry about it. Remind yourself that, if and when the event occurs, you have a plan and you will have the ability and resources to deal with it at the time.

If you're having negative thoughts about some misfortune that has occurred, think instead that, it's happened, you can't undo it, better learn from it, and look for any good or new opportunities that it may present.

If you're regretting a costly mistake that you've made, remind yourself that you did the best with the information you had, that it was worth the risk, that you're still fit and able, and that in short while you will recover from the problem that your mistake caused.

If you're thinking you want something that you can't have (a better car / house / job) replace it with the thought that once the novelty wore off you wouldn't be any happier if you had it, count your present blessings, and think about all the good things in your life

If you're jealous of someone who's just won a fortune, try feeling pleased for them instead.

Sometimes you may be able to reach a counter to a worrying thought by asking "so what if the worst possible outcome happened". Then having imagined the resulting worst scenario ask yourself "so what if the worst next outcome happened?". Sometimes this will lead you to realise that you could cope with even the worst and most unlikely series of outcomes to your concern, so you stop worrying about it.

Make the habit, every time you are aware of a recurring negative thought try and replace it with a positive counter thought. □

UR1.4. Learn to Generate and Foster Positive Thoughts

UR1.4.1 List Some Positive Thoughts

Spend time considering which are the most positive thoughts you can generate, and list them. Here are a few examples with which to prompt you. You will find more (for example *blog.gratefulness.me*).

- Gratitude for our loved ones, family and friends and for the love and support that we receive and give through our relationships
- Gratitude for all the good things in our life, for our health, for our livelihood, our food, shelter and our security.
- Gratitude for our upbringing and education in life and to all those who have helped us progress.
- Gratitude for our life so far and for our past experiences, pleasures, achievements and progress.

- Gratitude for our present sources of happiness
- Gratitude for the many good things in the world, and the many good people
- Gratitude for positive personal characteristics that others see in you.
- Recalling the most uplifting, exciting or satisfying experiences you've ever had
- Recalling the most uplifting places you've experienced or seen images of.
- Anticipation of future planned pleasant experiences and pleasures
- Imagining uplifting places that we enjoy
- Imagining uplifting experiences that we enjoy and people whose company we enjoy.
- Thoughts of love for the people dear to us

UR1.4.2 Foster Positive Thoughts

To train our plastic mind to think more positively we need to repeat these positive thoughts many times. So having generated a list of positive thoughts that suit you personally, find ways to foster those thoughts so that they will often recur. Some ideas are presented below to get you started.

Gratitude Linked Meditation

Gratitude seems to be a particularly powerful source of positive thoughts. Thoughts of gratitude can make us more content, more happy, more optimistic, and less greedy. They help us see the glass as half full not half empty. Here's one way to foster them; write a list of some of the things you are most grateful for. Even if you're in a bad situation try and think of the things that aren't bad and for which you're grateful. Read it several times and memorise the list, or at least the headings. Then after you have done one of your attention-based meditation sessions, while your mind is calm and clear, go through the list in your head and take time to feel grateful for each thing on the list, like a guided meditation. Make this a regular practice so as to foster these thoughts and notice how it makes you feel afterwards.

In a similar way, you can link a meditation session as a vehicle to consciously exercise other positive themes, such as sending love to your family, or going through a list of uplifting topics or places.

Other techniques

Here are some other commonly used methods of fostering positive thoughts. Experiment to find out which method suits you best.

- At the end of every day *write down* some things that happened for which you are grateful, even very small things.
- Write an *affirmation* (see books by *Louise L Hay* including *You Can Heal Your Life*) of messages to yourself and repeat this affirmation every day.
- Play suitable audio recordings (sometimes called *guided meditations*) that trigger positive thoughts.

- You can find *aspiration lists* and *guided meditations* that help you make various specific positive changes such as becoming more compassionate, reducing anger, managing pain, coping with grief.

(Note: In Appendix A4 that the model described there suggests that maybe our mind reacts in the same way to imagined images as it does to real world ones. That might be a clue as to why affirmations and visualisations work?)

UR2 Learn to Choose Positive Actions.

Introduction

Our thoughts determine our feelings and our actions. Our actions lead to consequences that can be beneficial or harmful and can make us happy or unhappy. In this section we focus on the importance of choosing positive actions. These include purposeful actions that keep our mind engaged, actions that uplift us, actions that lead us to new experiences, and harmful actions that we choose to avoid. If we can condition our minds to choose these more positive actions, then we will become happier.

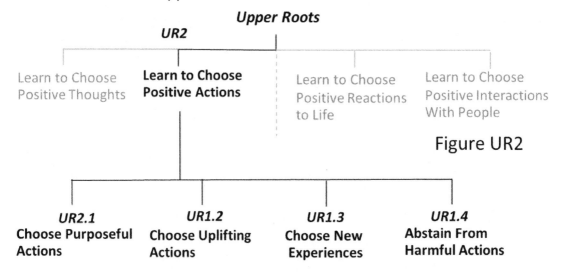

Figure UR2

UR2.1 Choose Purposeful Actions

Purposeful actions can be any of the activities that make up our lifestyle (as depicted in the branches of the tree). These includes work, leisure activities and hobbies, socialising, exercising, developing our mind and body, helping others, learning and teaching. Each of these activities brings its own rewards for example earning a living, job satisfaction, fun, social connection, uplifting experiences, physical wellbeing and so on. They are sources of happiness.

In addition, they all have another extremely important benefit: they keep our mind engaged, they keep us from boredom, and they reduce the time spent in idleness where we are prone to negative thinking. Being engaged in purposeful action makes us happier.

UR2.2 Choose Uplifting Actions

Each time we have an uplifting experience, even momentarily, it creates a positive feeling. Repetition helps us maintain a happier mood.

UR2.2.1 Enjoy Pleasures

We can be uplifted by any of the sensual pleasures. Look forward to them. Take time to savour them in the moment.

UR2.2.2 Enjoy Uplifting Places

We can deliberately choose to spend more time in environments that uplift us or appeal to our aesthetic sense. This could be in the countryside, by the sea, in mountains or in beautiful gardens, parks, towns or buildings. Conversely, we can attempt to spend less time in environments that depress us.

UR2.2.3 Create Uplifting Spaces

We don't always have the freedom to choose where we spend our time, but we mostly have the freedom to create a small uplifting space of our own to spend time in. For some this could be a room that we deliberately decorate and furnish with pictures, ornaments and personal souvenirs that uplift us. For others it might be creating a patio or garden with uplifting scents, colours and textures. For others it might be joining in a community project to make an uplifting space in the neighbourhood.

UR2.2.4 Spend Time with Uplifting People

We can choose to spend more time with people we find uplifting, and less with those who make us feel down (but remembering the need to help others).

UR2.2.5 Laugh

Humour uplifts us and makes us feel good. Laughing is good for us. Find ways to use technology to access comedy entertainment more easily. Next time you're unoccupied and tempted to look at the news on your phone, switch to a humorous video or comic show instead.

UR2.3 Explore New Experiences

We are born with a natural curiosity. We like to try new things; it's how we learn. As we get older, we learn to be more aware of danger and are less inclined to take risks. We then become more inclined to stay within our *comfort zone* and resist new experiences. We may get into a rut. We may feel we've seen it all before, or we may have believed the saying that "old dogs can't learn new tricks". We are in fact never too old to try new things and were never too old to learn. New experiences might include new activities, visiting new places, meeting new people, or opportunities for learning something new. New experiences refresh the mind, expand our model of the world, and can generates new ongoing interests. Travel broadens the mind. Taking on new challenges can give us a sense of achievement, and taking reasonable risks is part of being alive and may make us less fearful. If you are hesitant, you could team up with a friend to share the new experience together. This makes it even more rewarding.

UR2.4 Abstain from Negative Actions

UR2.4.1 Kamma

Learn that all actions have consequences, and that your present actions affect your future condition and happiness and that of others. This is the Buddhist teaching known as the law of Kamma. Choose to think about the consequences of your actions and refrain from those that you think are negative and likely to cause harm.

UR2.4.2 Choose Moral Actions

Across many religions and cultures, and also in Buddhism, the ethics and moral codes have some strong similarities at their core. Many of the common elements are also encapsulated in national secular laws because moral actions have been found to be the foundation of a harmonious society. If we can restrict ourselves to moral actions then we are less likely to provoke dissent, division, anger, and violence in our society. We thus play our part in contributing to a more harmonious society in which people feel more secure and can flourish. We also are less likely to harm others, ourselves, or the planet, and less likely to suffer feelings of remorse and regret.

Below is an *example* of a moral code (actual codes will vary across religions cultures and individuals).

Abstain from murder.
Abstain from physically or mentally abusing others.
Abstain from stealing.
Abstain from substance abuse.
Abstain from lying or misrepresenting the truth.
Abstain from livelihoods that harm or exploit others.
Minimise your negative impact on the Planet.

Note 1. 'Minimising your negative impact on the planet' has been suggested as an additional moral duty. It includes understanding how your actions impact the planet then making positive choices in your everyday life.
Note 2. In many religions and cultures there is also a moral restricting sexual behaviour. Because it varies so much and can be contentious, no such code has been explicitly written above.

UR2.4.3 Abstain from Greedy Actions

We are continually influenced and tempted to want more than we really need, and we become conditioned to want more and to believe that constantly acquiring more will make us happy. Reflect that this is a false model. Owning more of something does not make us happier. Some *retail therapy* is ok, but it is a temporary pleasure not a way to enduring happiness. If we all *want the earth*, then there will be no earth left. Ask yourself how many possessions do you really need? If you want the pleasure of buying something, but you don't really need it, try buying it for someone who does. This will not only help them, but will make you feel better for longer, help you to be more compassionate, less greedy, and produce less impact on the planet.

UR3 Learn to Choose Positive Reactions to Life.

Introduction

In LR2 and LR3 we suggested that our mind forms models of the world, and that some of these models may be false and make us unhappy if we cling to them. In this section we describe how to detach from some of these false models by learning to *accept life* as it really is, rather than how we would prefer it to be.

By reflecting on the realities of life, and practising acceptance, we can gradually disable the ability of our false models to generate a stream of negative thoughts in reaction to the world, our lives, and events that occur. We also become more resilient. This is part of the process of learning to cultivate or re-condition our minds and so generate greater inner happiness (fixing some of the *holes in our cup*).

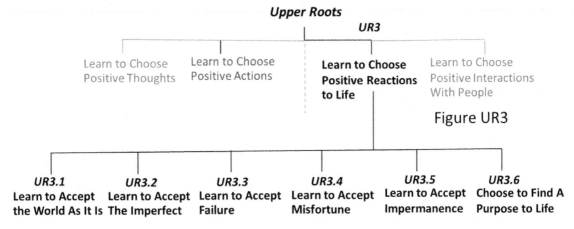

Figure UR3

UR3.1 Learn to Accept the World As It Is.

Learn to:

- Accept the world as it is and not how you would like it to be
- Accept that it doesn't and never will match up to your ideals
- Accept that there is much suffering in the world including poverty, sickness, violence, and death
- Accept that there are some people in the world who do very bad things and increase that suffering
- Accept that they sometimes cannot be stopped or punished
- Accept that the world is beyond your control, and that no one person controls it.

You may have good ideas, and think you know how everything should be done to improve the world. But, if you dwell too much on this, (playing at being God) then, even if your solutions are good, this will make you unhappy because you don't have the power to implement them.

You may at first think that acceptance seems like pessimism, defeatism, laziness, fatalism, or that it means not having ideals. Reflect instead that if you waste your energy thinking about things that you cannot influence, you have less energy to make positive changes in the areas where you can. So, focus on making improvements where you can, and be pleased with your achievement. (There may also be occasions where you can't do much to change the situation but can make a personal gesture such as writing a letter to a newspaper or donating to a relevant cause that you support).

Also recognise and be uplifted by all the *good* things that you experience in the world (for example the marvels of nature, the good people in the world, their beneficial acts).

UR3.2 Learn to Accept the Imperfect

If we have been taught to have high standards, we may believe that everything in the world, and everything we do, and everything in our life should be perfect. Every experience that isn't perfect becomes a disappointment. That makes life seem unsatisfactory and generates thoughts that make us unhappy.

If you recognize this tendency in yourself, try to lower your expectations. Stop being a perfectionist. Don't expect the world or your life to be perfect. Don't expect the outcomes of your efforts or other people's to be perfect. Don't expect everyday experiences or events that happen in your life to be perfect. Don't expect the material things that you acquire and use to be perfect. Don't require the outcomes of your decisions to be perfect. Choose instead to set realistic and achievable expectations. Choose to reflect on how good is " good enough". What if it's not perfect? Does it really matter? Ask yourself what's the downside to it not being perfect? Is there scope to improve it later? You will find that we don't often need something to be 100% perfect.

Reflect that if you realise when something is "good enough", then you will actually achieve more and get more done, because you won't be wasting time chasing perfection. You may find also that it helps you in making difficult choices and decisions.

This doesn't mean that you should be careless or lazy or produce or accept poor quality work. Nor does it mean that you shouldn't complain when you judge something acceptable.

UR3.3. Learn to Accept Failure

UR3.3.1 See Failure as Part of Learning

Reflect that we learned almost everything as children by trial and error. In learning to walk we made errors time and time again; every error made us stumble or fall and sometimes we hurt ourselves. Later we may have learned to ride a bike using the same process. Later again we may have learned other skills like playing an instrument or juggling. We don't think of each single error we made in learning these skills as a failure, we see the errors as a necessary part of learning.

When we think of bigger things that we undertake in our lives, like relationships, jobs, business ventures or any new personal initiatives that we make, we tend to see them in a different way. When we find we've made a mistake in such areas we see it as a 'big mistake', a failure, and this leads to self-recrimination, regret, unhappiness and can lead to depression.

You might reflect that if we saw our *'big'* mistakes in the same light as our *'small ones'* we might regard them also as having been learning opportunities. We might then, after our initial disappointment, find it a little easier to consider what we have learned and move on.

UR3.3.2 Accept That Your Plans Will Go Wrong
We can fool ourselves into thinking that everything should go as planned, and when it doesn't, we get disappointed. Planning is really important, it helps us to succeed in many ways, especially at work. But a plan isn't reality. We cannot see into the future; we make predictions or guesses based on what we know from the past. But our knowledge is invariably incomplete and *"we don't know what we don't know"*. So if we falsely cling to a plan as real then, when things don't go to plan, we get very disappointed.

In the same way we often have to make decisions without having all the knowledge of the likely outcome, so it follows that they may be wrong.

Accept that the processes of planning and decision making are imperfect, but reflect that the alternative is to do nothing, learn nothing and not progress.

UR3.3.3 See Failure as Part of the Path to Success
See failure as a necessary consequence of trying something new. It's bound to happen sometimes. There's always a risk of failure. It's not a reason to stop trying. Accept that risk is part of life. If you fear consequences too much you will never try anything new and you will get in a rut from staying in your comfort zone. Also, you can't avoid risk, even by doing nothing. For example, if you stayed in bed all day to be safe, you would suffer bone damage and muscle wastage. If you don't try, you cannot succeed. When you next experience failure, examine what you have learned from it. Then decide to either try again or change direction. Exploit any opportunity presented by what you have learned.
" The only failure is the failure to try ". " if at first you don't succeed, try, try again "

UR3.4 Learn to Accept Misfortune

UR3.4.1 Accept that Misfortune is Inevitable.
We all experience misfortune at times in our lives. We may get sick, have an accident, lose our job, be the victim of crime or of freak weather. These can very difficult to cope with and take time to come to terms with. After the event we may have recriminations, like *why did I / you let this happen, whose fault is it? How could I have avoided it?* We may have severe regrets over our actions and spend a long time reliving the event and blaming ourselves or others.

It may help to accept that the world is not under our control, and we cannot see into the future. Inevitably some misfortune will occur to us or our loved ones. It's not necessarily anyone's fault. It Happens.

UR3.4.2 See an Event in Its Context

Sometimes it can ease our unhappiness by seeing an event in context and reflecting on it for example;

- *I suppose I knew I was taking a risk, it had to happen sooner or later.*
- *I am old and I've been luckier than most till now*
- *It's not the end of the world, I can get over it and start again.*
- *It could have been much worse, I'm still here, I'm lucky compared to many*
- *I'll do better next time*
- *It's really bad, but everything else went ok*

UR3.4.3 Exploit Any Positive Side and Move On

Remember the saying *"every cloud has a silver lining "*. Look for any possible positive outcome and exploit it. For example, losing your job might spur you to find a better one. Being ill for a few weeks might give you time to read a book you've been intending to read, or give you pause to take stock of your life

UR3.5 Accept That Life is Not Permanent

Everything in the universe is temporary, everything is in the process of change. We ourselves and our loved ones will get old and sick and die. Nobody on earth is immune to that process. Our planet, our sun, the universe, all are in the process of change and won't exist forever in their present form.

Even though our rational mind knows this, we are averse to thinking about it, and since day-by-day changes are small, we tend not to notice them. We get on with our lives and ignore the fact that our time is limited, and that we don't know when we're going to die. We think and act as though we've got forever.

From time to time, we are reminded of our impermanence (the first grey hairs or wrinkles, the death of a relative) and it makes us very unhappy.

Buddhists believe that if we want to be happy it is better to face the reality of death and learn to accept it. This can help us make the most of the present. Some Buddhists make themselves more accepting of death by the nature of their funeral ceremonies and by regularly visiting crematoria. It helps them keep it in mind and be more accepting of their impermanence.

You might like to occasionally reflect on your impermanence. You might reflect on the fact that at some point in time you may not be able to do things that you now can, like walking, or visiting friends. Make up your mind to make the most of these abilities to enjoy life now while you still can. You might reflect on what you would likely be thinking when you die, and in consequence decide what things you might want to achieve before then. You might reflect on what your legacy of help to others will have been. You might decide to give more help now. You might reflect on things that you might wish to have said, particularly regarding thanks and apologies, and say them now.

UR3.6 Choose to Find a Purpose in Life

Note: Those readers who are religious may choose to ignore this section, though it is not in any way intended to challenge religious belief.

UR3.6.1 Our Quest for the Meaning of Life

In evolutionary theory the prime purpose of a species is to survive and reproduce. These purposes shape and drive the behaviour of each species, including humans. Much of what we think and do is directed by inbuilt mechanisms to fulfil these purposes or needs. (*Maslow, Freud*). The genes that we pass on through our children are our natural or genetic legacy.

But for the human species reproduction is not always enough of a mission statement. As we evolved our brains became more complex and we developed imagination and the power to analyse and to form models of the world. We developed the curiosity to ask questions and the thinking to find answers. We developed consciousness. Having developed these abilities it is not surprising that long ago we turned them on ourselves and our world. We started to ask who are we, what is our relationship to the world, why are we here, what is the meaning of life? And we still do. We search for a meaning in our lives and if we can can find one, it makes us stronger, more secure, and happier.

Religion, for many, provides an answer and has done so for thousands of years. Those who are religious have a faith that may help to give them a purpose and meaning to life.

If you are not religious, then it is not very uplifting to think that we are just a minor quirk of evolution, one species of many, on one tiny planet in a vast universe. Nor that our life terminates when we die, and that we are soon forgotten. Nor that all life on the planet will cease at some time when our sun burns out. Nor that many aspects of life and the universe appear to be complex beyond our understanding. We want to escape from the feelings of dissatisfaction, insignificance, and pointlessness that these thoughts can cause.

UR3.6.2 How Can We Find a Sense of Purpose?

There is no easy answer, and we are all different. A first step might be perhaps to think of the purposes behind all the present activities in your life. You will benefit if you recognise that your work has a purpose, that your time spent with loved ones has purpose, that your efforts raising your children has a purpose and so on. Maybe you can also consciously look at what drives other people, especially those that you respect, and learn from them. If you look around:

- You will see some whose purpose is to gain wealth, they want everything and then more
- You may see some people who are driven to want power, to be in charge, to rule the world
- You may see some whose purpose is to be famous, glamourous, and admired.
- You may see some whose main purpose is work, they have a calling, a very strong drive to do something useful, or to achieve something with their lives.
- You may see some who find their purpose to raise their children and give them a good start in life.
- You may see some who see their purpose as helping others

- And some who believe their highest need is altruism or spiritual connection to others, to nature, to other species and to the whole cosmos.

Maybe some of the threads that exist in this Happiness Tree model could help you find your own personal sense of meaning and purpose. For example, you might consider that:

- We are social animals, so, for most of us, people are the most important thing in our lives, and that whatever this life is, we're *all in it together.*
- If we were all a little bit nicer to each other the world would be a better place.
- That moral virtue and generosity lead to a more harmonious, happier society.
- That if we cultivate our minds, we lead happier lives and help others to be happier.

One way of looking at life is that:

The total of the little bits of help that you give others, is both your legacy and the purpose of your life.

In the Tree model this is depicted by the fruit on the tree. It is interesting to note that later in life Maslow added a new top layer to his pyramid of human needs. He called it altruism.

UR4 Learn to Choose Positive Interactions with People.

Introduction

In LR1 we learned that we evolved as social animals; we are inextricably linked to other people, we depend on them, they depend on us. People are arguably the most important aspect of our lives. Positive interactions with others increase harmonious living and make us all happier. Negative ones increase division and can lead to unhappiness and strife.

In LR2 and LR3 we learned that some negative interactions with others are caused by our preconditioned negative personal traits such as greed, meanness, jealousy etc. We also learned that one way to improve our interactions is to recognise these traits in ourselves and resolve to correct them. One way to do this is to practise doing the opposite. For example; practising compassion makes us less greedy, practising generosity makes us less mean, praising the success of others makes us less jealous.

We also learned that other negative interactions are rooted in our holding onto false models such as a belief that everyone (including ourselves) should be perfect. Other negative interactions may be rooted in our failure to understand that everybody's models are different, so what is acceptable to one is unacceptable to another.

If you can learn to become more aware of, and detach from these traits and false models, you gradually disable their ability to generate negative thoughts and interactions. You will have more positive interactions with other people (and self); you will become happier and you will also help others to become happier. This is part of the process of learning to cultivate or re-condition our minds.

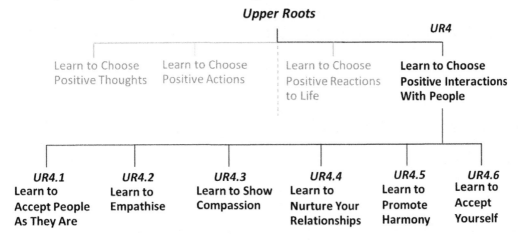

Figure UR4

UR4.1 Learn to Accept People as They Are.

Lower your expectations of other people. Do not continually expect them to be perfect, or to be like you, or to share your standards, or you will be continually disappointed.

Remember we all have different values and beliefs, remember that what is acceptable to others may be unacceptable to you, and vice versa.

Realise that you cannot change other people; they are the only ones who can change themselves. They may not see a need to do so, or may not be ready to, or may think it's you that should change. You will otherwise be frustrated that your well-intentioned efforts *"fall on stony ground"*. (This doesn't mean that you shouldn't try to help, but that you should realise that your advice may not be wanted or that it might be untimely).

UR4.2 Learn to Empathise.

When you engage with someone or observe their actions, try to suspend rapid judgement and the use of stereotypes. First impressions can be powerful and valuable but are not always reliable. So, if you are not in immediate danger, and you don't need a snap decision, pause a little.

Take time and try to learn a little more about the person, their situation, and the context. Explore their views and background, ask open questions. Above all, listen.

Try and see their point of view. Imagine what you would think if you were in their shoes. Try and understand what's behind their actions or opinions; how their experience has shaped their view, and why they think and act the way they do.

Reflect on your differing experiences and reactions and on whether you would act similarly in their situation.

An example (*from Prof Muesse*); when you encounter someone doing something that starts to irritate you (like holding up a shop queue because they can't find their credit card) instead of feeling angry with them, recognise that you have done similar things and think *"just like me"*.

UR4.3 Learn to Show Compassion.

UR4.3.1 Show Sympathy.

When you see someone who is suffering or in need, rather than being critical or judgemental, try to empathise with them and imagine how you would feel in their shoes. Demonstrate to them some sympathy and pity for their misfortune. Show some warmth by making contact through a kind word, a hug or polite gesture.

UR4.3.2 Show Kindness'

Try to find a way to help with material help, support or advice.

UR4.3.3 The benefits of compassion

It is obvious that the person you help benefits from your help (provided you helped wisely).

Helping is contagious. The person you helped is more likely to help others later. In addition, on occasions when your help is visible to others, they in turn may be influenced to follow your example.

If everyone chooses to give a bit of help, then the cumulative effect makes the world a better and happier place.

You will also benefit from helping others; it gives you a good feeling to know you helped someone (especially if you can see the result or get a thank you). Remember the saying: *"Virtue is its own reward."*

By showing compassion and helping others you become more likely to help again later, so you become a better person (in the same way that doing something bad can lead you to becoming a habitual criminal).

By helping others, you help yourself to be less greedy.

As discussed in UR3.6, one way of looking at life is that the sum total of the little bits of help that you gave others is both your legacy and the purpose of your life.

UR4.4 Learn to Nurture Your Relationships

Choose to *look for the good side* in others, don't just focus on the bad.

Give praise for the good you see in others. This will make your relationships more resilient.

Be a good listener. Allow others time to speak, don't seek to dominate others in your conversation or actions.

Show forgiveness when someone wrongs you. Harbouring a grudge, or wanting revenge, is corrosive to your mind, and can also lead to escalating strife.

Show gratitude when someone helps you. We don't always remember to do it; we may take acts of kindness for granted. Showing gratitude makes the person who helped you feel appreciated. Explicitly acknowledging the help makes you feel good as well.

Try to be open to new encounters. It's true that there may some people that you will encounter that you instinctively perceive as being a threat to you. But if you are too wary of everyone, then you may miss the opportunities for positive interactions with the majority of people who are not a threat to you. So, be friendly and open to those you meet in your everyday life. Make eye contact and smile. Don't let shyness prevent you from being the first one to *open a conversation*. This has many benefits. It can make you and the other person more cheery and it can be a pleasant way to pass the time, for example when waiting in a queue or travelling. It can help distract you from boredom and negative thinking. You may find that there are ways that you can help each other. You may even sometimes learn something important that you would otherwise not have found out.

UR4.5 Promote Harmony

UR4.5.1 Choose Moral Speech and Writing.

If we can restrict ourselves to moral speech (and writing) then we are less likely to provoke dissent, division, and anger in our society. We thus play our part in contributing to a more harmonious society.

Moral Speech and Writing refers to that which is true, useful, polite, timely and kindly in intent and is free from ;

- lying (intentionally misrepresenting the truth)
- slander and libel
- divisive words (intended to break up or undermine friendships or potential friendships)
- harsh or unkindly words (intended to hurt someone's feelings)
- malicious gossip

UR4.5.2 Preempt Conflict

Highlight potential areas of conflict. This can be done in a way that is assertive but not aggressive, and which informs the other party of how some aspect of their behaviour is making you or others feel unhappy. You may feel intimidated or be reluctant to make a fuss. But if the matter is seriously upsetting you, and you suppress your concerns, you, are likely to get either very unhappy or progressively more angry and eventually overreact.

Negotiate, explain what you would like, listen to the other party, try to see their point of view and context. Try to find common ground and reach an agreement where possible. Sometimes a conciliatory gesture is helpful. If you don't know the other party you may want to find out more about them, for instance what are their priorities and problems and whether they are likely to be honest in negotiation.

If no agreement is possible, you can *'agree to differ'* and find coping strategies, or you may seek help from a neutral third party to arbitrate. If you can, learn to read *body language* and become more conscious of your own. This can help in negotiations.

UR4.5.3 Manage Your Anger

We respond to some actions or events with anger. This is a normal emotive response and probably serves some evolutionary need. For example, a degree of anger produces body language that may visibly communicate to someone that we find their behaviour unacceptable and want them to stop. However, if the anger is not controlled it can produce a response that escalates to conflict. If an individual gets angry too easily or too violently then this becomes a corrosive influence on relationships and communities.

Impatience often provokes anger. It is often helpful to take a break, count to ten then reflect on what has happened, and try to defuse and resolve the problem. Learning to empathise and negotiate can also help. There are books and courses available on anger management.

UR4.6 Learn to Accept Yourself

UR4.6.1 Lower Unrealistic Expectations

Some people have a low opinion of themselves, they have low self-esteem and lack self- confidence. This may involve recurring negative thoughts such as *I'm too big, too small, too fat, too thin, not pretty, or handsome enough, not clever enough, not brave enough, not strong enough, not successful enough.* This might be viewed as a form of perfectionism that we are unaware of. We constantly compare ourselves with others, or with some imaginary model of a perfect person and of course we keep failing the test because we've set the standards too high. The solution is to lower our expectations, but because it's our view of *self* that's in question, we find that difficult to do. Every time one of these self-critical thoughts occurs, it becomes more embedded, and we believe it more strongly. This nagging inner voice makes us unhappy, makes us under confident and shy, and leads us not to try things because we assume we're not up to it. So how can we lower our expectations and increase our self-esteem?

UR4.6.2 Some Tips

Recognise your good points and keep reminding yourself of them. Feel grateful for them, make an affirmation about them, repeat it often.

Find out how your friends see you; you might be surprised. They wouldn't dream of expecting you to be perfect in every way, they like and accept you as you are. Can you not trust their judgement?

Reflect on how others (family, friends, colleagues) respect your contribution to life. Are they all wrong?

Reflect on this supposed "person " that you aspire to be, and you may realise that in all the world there has never been anyone who has combined all the qualities that you wish for yourself. (You may be combining many role models into one superhero, who is perfect in every intellectual, emotional and physical respect but has never existed). Everyone has their strengths and weaknesses and so have you. Remember that: *"Comparison is the thief of Joy"*.

Learn to accept yourself as you are rather than endlessly regretting that you're not perfect in every way

Choose not to dwell on self, detach from it. Look from outside, see yourself getting on with your life, just like everyone else in the picture, doing the best you can with what you've been given. Your close attachment to the concept of *self* may be contributing to the problem. If you need help there are books and courses available.

Remember that most human activities and achievements rely on teamworking between individuals with differing strengths and weaknesses, none of whom are perfect. Also, reflect that all achievements are made by imperfect people.

Part 4.The Branches. Choose to Grow a Happier, Healthier Lifestyle.

Introduction

The branches of the tree represent your lifestyle. They have been chosen to reflect recognisably different aspects of everyday life (work, rest, play, family etc) in a structure that is also consistent with the roots of the tree.

The lifestyle choices that you make, directly affect your happiness and health (and in some cases your wealth). The branches include activities that are your external sources of happiness (job satisfaction, positive relationships, pleasurable pursuits, etc.).

The Branches have been split into levels for ease of presentation, as shown in Figure1.6.

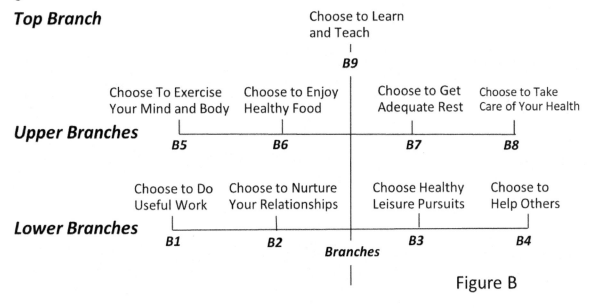

Figure B

The Lower Branches B1-B4 are as follows; B1 addresses work, B2 relationships, B3 leisure and B4 helping others.

The Upper Branches B5-B8 have a common theme relating to lifestyle choices that help maintain your *health and wellbeing*. B5 is about exercise and development including mind- body practices, B6 is about eating healthily, B7 is about Rest and B8 is about various aspects of protecting your health.

The Top Branch B9 is about learning and teaching.

The educational material in the branches is intended to help us make positive lifestyle choices (like healthy eating). It can also include advice on how to implement that choice (e.g. learning to cook healthy food).

B 1 Choose to Do Useful Work

Introduction
In this section we talk about some types of work and the benefits that work brings us and some of the pitfalls to avoid. Work is one of the lifestyle activities that relates to the root UR 2.1 *'Choose Actions With Purpose'*

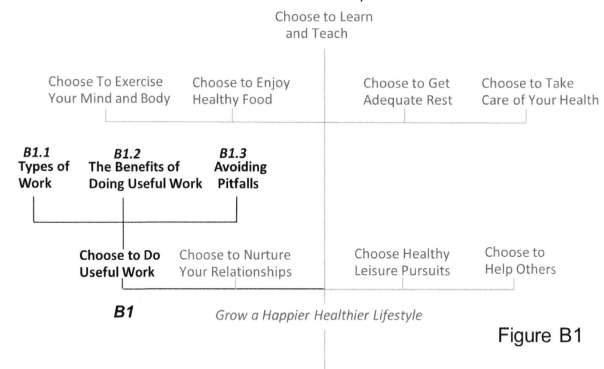

Figure B1

B1.1 Types of Work
We choose here to divide work into three categories,

     1 Job or livelihood (earning a living)
     2 Household Work
     3 Raising Children.

These subdivisions can be applied across very different cultures. For example, in a hunter gatherer tribe they would correspond to 1. hunting and gathering food and materials; 2. making a shelter, cooking food, making tools and clothes; 3. raising children. In a western city dweller, they might correspond to; 1. a paid job 2. DIY, gardening, shopping, cooking, household finances; 3. raising children.

B1.1.1 Job
There are many different types of job covering a whole spectrum of activities, for example subsistence farmer, agricultural worker, teacher, brain surgeon, builder, shopkeeper, gardener, driver, factory worker, scientist.

     There are also categories like employee, self-employed, full time, part time, folio, casual, work from home, commuter, voluntary worker.

All these jobs (except voluntary worker) have a common benefit. They enable the person doing the job to earn payment, in money or in kind, to pay for food, shelter, family, material possessions etc. They provide a *livelihood*. However, they often have many other benefits (see B1.2 below).

B1.1.2 Household Work
This typically includes general maintenance of house, garden, and equipment (eg car, lawnmower, bicycle etc.), as well as shopping, cooking, financial and household management (paying bills, taxes, general admin).

B1.1.3 Raising Children
It may seem odd to class this activity as work, because we do it for love, and it produces an entirely different kind of reward. But it is an activity with an extremely important purpose. It takes time and effort and requires skill. It fully engages our mind so here we put it in the same category as work.

B1.2 The Benefits of Doing Useful Work
- When we are working our mind is engaged, and we are less prone to negative thoughts and are therefore generally happier.
- An interesting job can give us opportunity for new experiences and challenges and keep our mind active.
- A job gives us vital social contact, and gets us out of the house
- It also provides some sort of routine, structure, and a sense of purpose.
- Working in a team makes us feel good.
- We get job satisfaction, a sense of achievement from a job well done, or a challenge overcome.
- When others recognise that we have done a good job, this can increase our self-esteem.
- A job may give us opportunities for learning, and personal development. We may learn specialist skills as well as transferable ones such as interpersonal, management and communication skills.
- A job may give us opportunities to teach others what we have learned and help them develop.
- The products of our work benefit our customers / society as a whole and this can also make us feel good.
- Some people are fortunate enough to have a vocational job or an interesting job which they enjoy. But a job doesn't have to be very interesting or high status or well paid to make us happy.
- Doing household work provides the benefit of tasty food and a clean comfortable place to live. For some people cooking and DIY also become an interest or hobby, and a chance to learn.
- The benefits of the efforts put in to raising children are of a different nature. They are more personal and emotional. They include great joy and love. For many people giving their children a good upbringing and a good start in life is one of their most important tasks and most rewarding experiences.

Their effort is also a crucial benefit to society as a whole. If this task is neglected, then not only do the child and parents become unhappy but there is a risk that the child will later in life do things that are harmful to others and make society as a whole less happy.

B1.3 Avoiding Pitfalls

B1.3.1 Protect Your Health
When working, be aware of any hazards and take precautions to protect your safety and your health.

Work within the relevant official health and safety guidelines and regulations.

If your work is very stressful, seek ways to manage the stress and periodically relax.

B1.3.2 Avoid Prolonged Overworking
There will often be externally or internally generated pressures to work longer and harder. We may have to meet a deadline or maybe were driven by urge to finish a task. We can cope with this, we may even enjoy the challenge. But if we overwork for long enough the pressure can take a toll on our physical and mental health. Prolonged physical effort without enough rest means that our body doesn't get time to do its own repair and maintenance. Prolonged mental stress keeps our cortisol levels high leading to ill health. Prolonged mental effort, especially if it's intellectually demanding, can lead to nervous exhaustion. Maybe our brain chemicals get depleted. We don't usually see it coming but it can suddenly hit us and leave us depressed, then we are forced to stop for a long time.

In Japan, there is a strong cultural work ethic that sometimes leads to sudden death (heart attack, stroke) from overworking. They have a word for it: *Karoshi.*

Bear in mind that when you overwork you are also spending less time with loved ones and less time in recreational pursuits and less time resting, so it's a twofold problem. Bear in mind also that over-work can become addictive.

B1.3.3 Remember to Throw the Work / Life Switch
This means more than just *" not taking work home "* It means also having a different mindset in your personal life to the one that you use at work. It means for example that in your personal life you switch off processes like measuring, comparing, analysing, predicting, planning, and avoiding risk. These processes can be very beneficial at work but will make you unhappy if you apply them in your personal life.

B1.3.4 Choose not to Procrastinate.
Sometimes we may repeatedly delay doing a particular job because we are averse to it. The very thought of it makes us feel unhappy so we distract ourselves with a more pleasant job. But if we defer a job that is necessary, then the thought of it will keep coming back. We can't escape it. The longer we put it

off the more times we get to be made to feel bad. Even worse the repeated thinking about it makes the task seem more daunting. And, of course, we eventually run out of time.

Here are some tips;-

Promise you'll spend just 5 minutes on it to make a start, but that you'll do it now, not later. Sometimes, after you've done 5 minutes, you will find the job isn't as bad as you thought, and you go on to finish it.

If it's a very big job, then that may stop you from starting it. So, promise yourself that you will spend say 1 hour a day on it. Breaking it up into bits that makes it easier to manage

B1.4 Career Development

B1.4.1 Develop and Use Your Interpersonal Skills

If you learn to apply the skills described previously in UR4 then your interactions with all the people you engage with at work will be improved (colleagues, superiors, subordinates, customers, suppliers). This will not only make your work more enjoyable, but will make you a more valuable team member, and so enhance your career prospects.

Wherever possible make the effort to be open to contacts and to develop a network of relationships not only in your immediate group but across departmental or organizational boundaries. You may be surprised at how well this network keeps you informed about everything that is going on. This helps you understand how the organization actually works (and areas where it doesn't). This also can make you a more valued team member and can help you identify career opportunities.

B1.4.2 Career Change

It pays to take stock occasionally of your list of skills, update your CV, talk to your network of friends and colleagues, keep an eye open for new possibilities, and take advantage of any opportunities that arise. This includes looking for promotion within your current organisation as well as opportunities elsewhere.

Take advantage of training opportunities that may arise so as to learn useful new skills to enhance your CV.

There's an interesting Japanese technique called 'Ikigai' that you could try if you are thinking of a career change. It's based on a simple picture model, and is claimed to help you navigate important career and life decisions. (Melanie Wilding, Betterhumans.pub, LMSW Nov 30, 2017). You could also use it to plan a retirement activity or a paying hobby.

Don't get in a rut. You may not like your job but have decided to stay with it just because you think it's all you know how to do. But people often acquire many *"transferable skills"*, that would be equally valid in a different type of job. You may have many skills that would transfer to a different job, but be unaware of them, so it pays to take stock of them occasionally by updating your CV.

B1.4.3 Redundancy

This can be devastating. Apart from the financial impact, you lose at a stroke the social contacts and all the other benefits of working. At such a time it's important to remember that you probably have more general *transferable skills* than you realise, and so you shouldn't rule out going in a different direction or exploiting a new opportunity.

B1.4.4 Retirement

Some people love their work too much to retire, and if they are fortunate enough to have a choice they keep going, sometimes in a part time role, or in a teaching role where they can pass on their experience.

Some who have less interesting jobs or stressful or physically demanding jobs look forward very much to retirement, only to find that they get bored and miss work when they retire, especially the social contact. It is important, if you are going to retire, to develop substitute activities that give you some of the benefits of work (e.g. learning a new skill, getting an undemanding part time job, voluntary work, sociable hobbies, something that gets you out of the house). Going part time can be a good stepping-stone to retirement. The *Ikigai* technique referred to above could be a valuable aid in making these important life decisions.

B2 Choose to Nurture Your Relationships

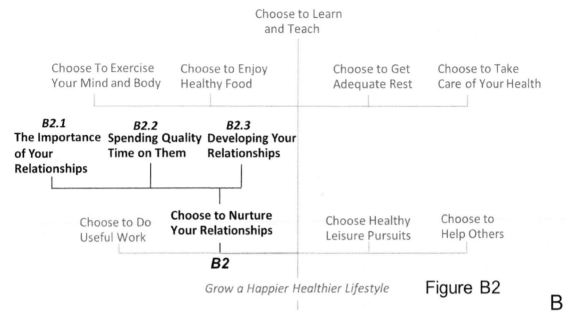

Grow a Happier Healthier Lifestyle   Figure B2

B

2.1 Recognise the Importance of Your Relationships

We evolved as social animals, so for most of us, people are the most important aspect of our lives. Our relationships and social contacts are an essential part of being human and directly affect our level of happiness and that of our loved ones and friends. We can draw and give happiness and strength from good relationships. Bad relationships drain our happiness and that of others. Isolation makes most of us very unhappy. It is not a surprise that solitary confinement is sometimes used as a form of punishment. We therefore need to *recognise* the important role of our relationships, in order to motivate ourselves to nurture and develop them.

B2.2 Spend Quality Time on Your Close Relationships

We have to balance our lifestyles. If we spend too much time at work, or at play, or are away from home too often then we risk neglecting our family relationships, and so losing some of the benefits. Similarly, if we don't make the effort to keep in touch with friends, then the friendships can fade. If we spend the time, and are good listeners, then we will also find out where we can usefully give help or support, or where we need to make changes in our own behaviour.

B2.3 Nurturing Your Relationships

We can nurture our relationships by choosing positive interactions as described previously in *UR4*.

We can do this by showing acceptance, by showing empathy, by recognising the good side as well as the bad in others, by not expecting perfection, and by showing praise, gratitude, and forgiveness, where due.

We can also help by using kindly speech and actions, and by being generous with our help and support.

To live harmoniously requires give and take. Sometimes we have to compromise and seek common ground and be patient. We should not seek to be dominant neither to be passive. We can be assertive but not aggressive and negotiate where needed.

Sometimes in the heat of the moment we may get angry and say hurtful things or react badly. It is important that we subsequently apologise and learn from what happened. Equally, if we are hurt it is important that we say so, but that we forgive and don't bear a grudge.

Sometimes if you are very unhappy you need to talk about it, and you may be greatly comforted by having someone you can openly talk to with. Remember this later when someone needs to talk to you.

Our relationships with children require particular skills. (Their minds and bodies are not mature. Their future behaviour and happiness depend greatly on what they learn from their interactions with us). There are many published resources which may help you.

B2.4 Develop New Relationships

Life continually changes, as do we. It is rewarding to continue to develop new relationships as we go through life. We described in section UR4.4 how this can be more easily done if you take opportunities to try new things and go to new places and are open and friendly towards the people you encounter. You can also develop friendships from work and from play.

B 3 Choose Healthy, Uplifting Leisure Pursuits

Introduction

This section deals with having fun and enjoying our leisure time. Our recreational pastimes can play an important part in our happiness and our physical and mental wellbeing. There are many pastimes to choose from and they vary across the world . Here we just mention a few common types and their benefits.

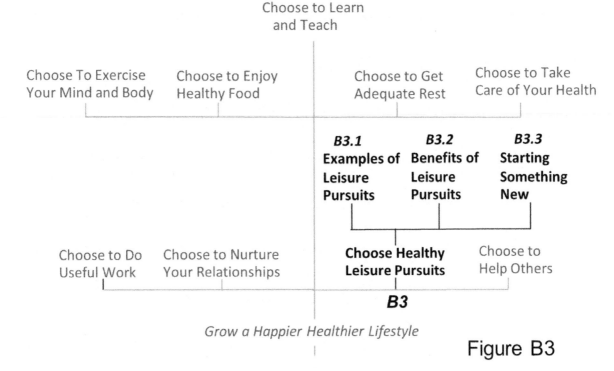

Figure B3

B3.1 Examples of Leisure Pursuits

The list is endless, and will vary with age, location and culture. Here is just a sample to illustrate what we're talking about. The subdivisions are arbitrary:-

Entertainment (tv,movies, comedy, online videos, mobile apps, eating out, theatre, music)
Hobbies (DIY, painting, reading, cookery, gardening, pets)
Sports (football, sailing, athletics, bowls)
Games (computer games, board games, quizzes)
Physical (walking, cycling, swimming, gym, yoga, dancing)
Travel (holidays, touring, camping)

B3.2 The Benefits of Leisure Pursuits

Prolonged working can lead to nervous exhaustion and unhappiness. Even if we lead busy lives, it benefits us to find time to fit in some leisure activity to distract us. We need such breaks to relax and refresh us and give our mind and body a rest. Some pastimes, like watching movies or comedy shows are relatively passive, but are relaxing and welcome distractions. Many other leisure pursuits are activities with some specific purpose. They don't involve the constraints or stress that can be associated with work, yet they keep the mind engaged and so reduce time spent ruminating and having negative thoughts. They can also provide exhilaration, uplift, enjoyment, fun, humour, and a sense of achievement. Some have additional benefits like social contact and team working. Others help keep us mentally and physically fit and resilient. Still others, like travel, provide us opportunities to meet people and try things outside of our normal experience. Our leisure activities help re-condition our mind with new experiences and so help us stay refreshed.

B3.3 Starting Something New

When choosing new activities, we may be tempted to think *"no I wouldn't enjoy that"* or *"thats not my sort of thing"*. In reality we don't know for sure till we give it a try. We need some novelty and variety in our lives to stay happy and avoid getting in a rut. Its better to *"give it a try"*. Sometimes it's good fun to try something new in company with a friend and share the fun.

Bear in mind that some activities have more than one benefit, for example taking the dog for an energetic walk, in beautiful countryside, in the company of friends.

B 4. Choose to Help Others.

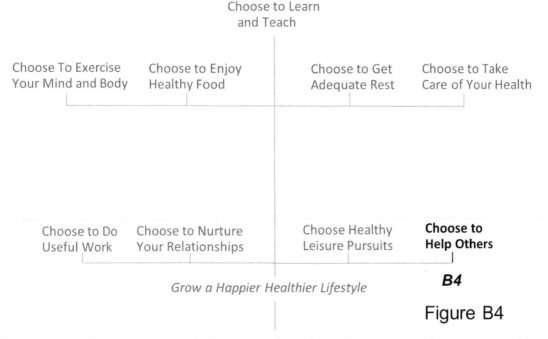

Figure B4

We discussed learned in *UR4.3* the benefits of helping others. Here we consider some types of help that you might choose to give:

You can give help directly to friends and family or people you meet that are in need. You can also help at a distance by supporting charities, shops, and other organisations that help good causes. Sometimes a little help at the right time can go a long way. Helping young people has a magnified benefit if it contributes to helping them grow into better, happier adults. Help can be a long-term investment that helps the recipients to help themselves more effectively in the future.

Help can take many forms. It can be supplying money, food, shelter, or material. But it can also be a kind or cheery word, a helping hand, some encouragement, or helpful advice. It can be teaching someone how to do something. You can also help by giving your time, by voluntary work or by fundraising. Sometimes, you can help someone by just being there for them, by providing a bit of company or being a good listener. You may even help someone unknowingly by being a role model. And of course, you can choose to help the community or the planet.

Maybe you can start by thinking about the best kind of help you can give, for example: what do you have to give? which causes strike a chord with you? and what best fits your lifestyle?. Look around, see what others are doing. Maybe you could start by joining in with friends on a shared venture. In this way you may also get to have fun, meet new people, and feel more joined up with your community, as well as getting all the other rewards of being compassionate.

Finally, you can help when you die by leaving a legacy that helps others.

B5 Choose to Exercise Your Mind and Body

Introduction

This is a very extensive subject, well covered elsewhere. A very simplistic summary is given below, just sufficient to give an overview and signpost the reader to the wealth of more detailed and authoritative material already available.

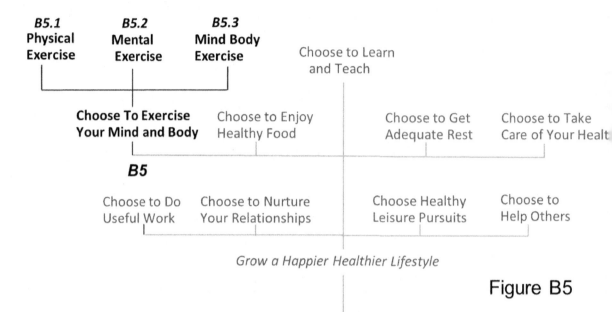

Figure B5

B 5.1 Physical Exercise

B5.1.1 The Benefits of Exercise

One of the few things that all health experts agree unanimously on is that exercise is good for us. It has been and still is a subject of extensive research. There is a wealth of evidence which shows that it's good for our mental and physical health, our resilience, and gives us an increased sense of wellbeing. Exercise can also help make us less vulnerable to some of the problems that we associate with old age, (for example, a bad back or poor balance).

Exercise triggers what we might call an *"Exercise Response "* that produces many beneficial changes in our brain and body. The nature of these changes is wide ranging and complex and beyond the scope of this book, but it is worth noting here that many people find that exercise makes them feel good afterwards. According to Julia Ross (*the Mood Cure*), this is because it allows more of the neurotransmitter *serotonin* to cross the blood brain barrier. It is the resulting increased level of serotonin in our brain that makes us feel good.

It has been commonly thought that exercise was an important contribution to weight loss, following the plausible argument of *calories in versus calories out*. More recently it has been found (for various reasons) that exercise does not seem to help us lose weight, and that for weight loss its best to focus on what we eat. (*Prof Tim Spector The Diet Myth*). You should not let that put you off exercise because there is overwhelming evidence that it is good for your health, your microbiome, your mood, and your life expectancy.

B5.1.2 Types of Physical Exercise

Exercise is often categorised as *aerobic* (burning lots of air and energy) or *anaerobic* (exerting a large force over small distance).

- *Aerobic exercises*, such as cycling, running, swimming, and walking, raise our heart rate and breathing rate which is particularly beneficial to heart and lungs but also benefits our whole body (and mind). It also benefits our circulation and increases our endurance.
- *Anaerobic exercise* such as lifting weights or using resistance bands develops increased strength, and keeps our muscles " in good shape", and our bones strong.
- A third form of exercise, which should be practised before and after the others, is *stretching*. This one is perhaps neglected more often than the others. Stretching helps keep our body flexible and resilient by lengthening the muscles tendons and ligaments and by making our joints go through their whole range of movement
- A fourth form of exercise involves *balance training.* Stretching and balance training make us less prone to falls and injury.

There are many different exercise formats, old and new, which combine elements of the above types of exercise. For example, *Pilates* is a relatively modern format that involves both stretching and strength training and includes aspects of Yoga.

We get some exercise in our daily activities but for many of us, that's not enough, especially if we're sat at a desk all day. It's a good idea to make exercise a part of your lifestyle.

There are many ways to exercise. We can exercise at home, at a gym, indoors or outdoors, or by taking up a sport. Sport has the advantage that because we enjoy it, we are more motivated to do it and the exercise comes as a bonus. You can sample different activities to find which suits you best or which ones that you enjoy most. You don't need expensive equipment to get going and you don't need to be young or be an athlete. The main thing is to just do it and make it part of your routine. There's a vast resource of information and equipment to help you.

B5.2 Mental Exercise

You may have to use your brain a lot every day at work. But if you don't then you can use puzzles and games such as crosswords, sudoku, riddles, anagrams, card games and board games such as chess. These exercise your brain in terms of your memory, and mental agility and flexibility. These can form an entertaining distraction to add to your routine. Using your brain also burns calories.

B5.3 Mind-Body Exercise

B5.3.1 Meditation and Mindfulness

The **most important place to start** is with the practice of meditation and mindfulness as already described in *UR1*. Make this a fixed part of your routine and persevere with it.

B5.3.2 Yoga

Another beneficial mind-body exercise is Yoga. This has its origins in India more than 5000 years ago and was associated with *Hinduism*. It was more a spiritual philosophy than a physical exercise. Some aspects have much in common with Buddhism. The word *yoga* comes from the Sanskrit word *'yuj'* meaning *'to centre one's thoughts'.* It was first documented by Patanjali who wrote the *Yoga Sutras* about 5000 years ago. This described the eight *limbs* of yoga (in a similar but different way that Buddha described the eightfold path). In the early 20th century Indian Gurus introduced Yoga to the west. By the 1980's one particular *limb* of yoga had become very popular in the west. This was the *asanas* or postures. This is what most of us think of today when we hear the word *yoga.* The *asanas* have subsequently further evolved into different styles. *Ashtanga* is the form described in the original sutras. *Hatha* yoga is a combination of meditation, breathing and postures. Then there are *Bikram, Kundalini, Vinyasa, Restorative* and other forms, each with special goals or emphasis. There is also a shortened set of exercises called *The Five Tibetans.*

Performing the yoga postures provides both aerobic and anaerobic exercise. It also increases flexibility, strength, vitality, posture and balance. Yoga also triggers the "relaxation response" to promote healing, and massages internal organs to promote detoxification. Like meditation, yoga teaches us to attend to our breathing and can be used as a way to calm the mind and focus inwards in a form of meditation. Many who try yoga find the benefits significant enough to continue long term.

B5.3.3 Tai Chi and Qigong

These forms of mind- body practice are both derived from ancient Chinese practices. They have their roots in martial arts, healing and meditation. They are now becoming increasingly popular in the West with local classes widely available, as well as DVDs.

Both forms typically involve sequences and repetitions of slow gentle movements of the limbs, while also focusing on the breath and concentrating the mind. They are usually carried out standing but can be adapted to a sitting position. They do not require great strength, fitness, or flexibility to make a start. They can be carried out equally well by young or old. Like Yoga, they are said to bring a range of physical and mental benefits. Specific exercise sequences have been devised by some teachers to benefit specific conditions such as arthritis.

It's not totally clear why or how the benefits are achieved but it's said that the practice promotes *circulation*. This doesn't just mean circulation of the blood.

In Traditional Chinese Medicine (TCM) emphasis is given to the flow of a field of energy in the body which is called *Qi* or *Chi* (sometimes called bioenergy or bio-electric energy). The various exercises involved in Tai-Chi and Qigong are said to bring benefits by stimulating the circulation or flow of this energy.

B5.3.4 Other Forms of Mind Body Exercise

There are other activities such as cold-water swimming that might be considered to be a mind-body exercise because they focus attention, in the moment, on the senses whilst at the same time exercising the circulatory system. Techniques to stimulate the *Vagus* nerve (by slow breathing, or by sound or pressure) might arguably also fall into this category.

B6 Choose to Enjoy Healthy Food

Introduction

The type and quantity of food we eat has a direct but not immediately visible effect on our health. *("You are what you eat", "Let food be thy medicine")*. Eating some foods can make us get sick more easily. It's harder to be happy when you are sick. Also, it's thought that some foods affect our mental health and moods directly. The subject of what is or isn't healthy food is a controversial and complex subject but a very important one. The author is not an expert but attempts here to shed some light on the subject, and produce a simple summary guide list. Rather than refer to individual research papers to support this work, he has chosen instead to cite expert authors who, in their books, cite relevant research. Because the subject is contentious, some readers may choose instead to go direct to authoritative sources and draw their own conclusions.

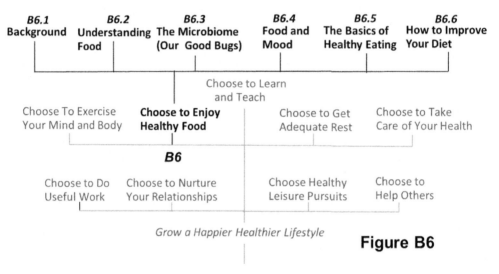

Figure B6

B 6.1 Background

Enjoying good food is something that is celebrated in cultures all around the world. For those of us fortunate enough to have enough food, it not only provides our energy and nourishes us, but it can be a source of great pleasure. Traditionally, in most cultures, considerable care and pleasure is taken in selecting the raw food material, and then in preparing and cooking it. Eating communally provides a natural and enjoyable focus for family and social interaction and is an important part of the fabric of society.

The type of food we eat, and the ways in which we cook it, varies enormously across different countries and cultures. It has also, in some countries varied through history as social conditions, farming, and technology has changed.

In recent times, particularly in some Western industrialised countries, there has been a recent rapid change in the type of food we eat. Many people now eat a diet that includes a higher amount of *processed* food rather than *natural* food. This trend started in the US, but other countries, including the UK, soon followed.

This change has occurred over a period of only 50 years or so. For many of us, much of the food that we buy is now delivered to the shop from a factory rather than from a farmer (or fisherman). Busy lifestyles may have contributed to making many of us less willing to devote time to the preparation of natural food, and the food industry has evolved to give us an easier option in the form of this fast, convenient and tasty *processed* food.

During roughly the same period of time that this dietary trend has occurred, there has been a large increase in the incidence of a number of serious health problems. The list includes obesity, diabetes type 2, heart disease, stroke, cancer, arthritis and depression. Is this a coincidence?

During this same period there has been a gradual increase in the size of the average waistline, coupled with a surge of interest in diets for weight loss. Is this a coincidence?

Throughout this period, scientists and health professionals have carried out extensive research and done their best to provide us with reliable advice as to what we should eat to stay healthy and /or lose weight. However, for various good reasons, the advice has been inconsistent, incomplete and in some cases wrong.

For example, at various times we've been told about the benefits of calorie counting, exercise, high fibre, low sugar, low fat, low carbs, high carbs, high protein and more recently 5 a day. Specific diets have been promoted including the Atkins diet, the Dukans diet, the Low GI diet, the Paleo diet, the Mediterranean diet the Keto diet and many more.

It's confusing, and small wonder that we have become in general somewhat sceptical about the subject. There may never have been a time where it is so important for individuals to learn about healthy nutrition, nor a time when it has been a more contentious subject.

In his book *The Diet Myth; the Real Science Behind What We Eat*, Professor Tim Spector gives a highly valuable, up to date and readable overview of the subject, based on cutting edge research. As a Professor of Genetic Epidemiology at Kings College London, and Honorary Consultant Physician at Guy's and St Thomas's Hospital, and author of over 700 papers on the subject of nutrition, he is eminently well placed to inform us, and his book is well worth a read.

According to Tim Spector, (sometimes referred to below as TS), there are several reasons why the earlier scientific research produced inconsistent results. In summary these included the facts that:

- The topic is inherently very complex, with many variables to account for, so the trials need to be particularly rigorous, and the results viewed in context (as part of the bigger picture).
- As individuals we are all genetically different.
- Regional groups can have genetic modifications due to their historical diet.

- Previous research didn't take into account the influence of our microbiome (the bugs inside us) whose huge importance is only recently begun to be understood (see below B6.3).

The good news from his book is that the new research is beginning to point in a more consistent direction. He explains how current research is very clearly and consistently showing us that **processed food is bad for us** and that **natural food is good for us**. It also points us towards a more **plant and mushroom based diet,** (vegetables, fruit, seeds, wholegrains, nuts and mushrooms) with only a smaller part of our diet coming from meat, fish and other **animal based products**. This mixed natural food regime is similar to that which our *hunter gatherer* ancestors are thought to have eaten for a million years or so. (To use an engineering analogy, you could say that it's the sort of food that we have been *"designed"* by evolution to eat and thrive on).

Many studies have explored the so-called *French Paradox* and concluded that the *Mediterranean Diet* seems to be the healthiest diet around today. It is a good example of the mixed, natural food-based regime described above.

Increasingly research is also pointing to the healing and preventive action of many of the compounds called phytonutrients (or phytochemicals) found in plants, vegetables and herbs (see *The Green Pharmacy* by *Dr James Duke*). This serves to reinforce the need for a significant part of our diet to be plant based.

In what follows, the author has drawn on material from *TS The Diet Myth* and also drawn on information from books by Chris Woollams (*The Rainbow Diet and How it Can Help You Beat Cancer*) and from many other sources on nutrition.

B6.2 Understanding Food

In order to make positive changes to our diet it may help to understand where our food comes from and what it contains. In the following pages below we describe the three different natural sources of food, and the three main components that they contain.

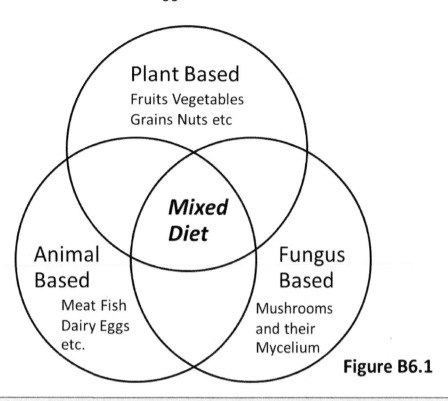

Figure B6.1

This shows the three sources of our food, Plant, Animal and Fungus based.
A ***Mixed Diet*** includes components from each source.

B6.2.1 Our Natural Sources of Food

We can describe our of food as coming from three natural sources as shown in Figure B6.1. These are

> *plant based.*
> > fruit and vegetables, including roots, leaves, skins, stems, flowers, nuts, seeds, grains, berries, pips, shoots, sprouts, micro-greens, oils and extracts, seaweed.
>
> *animal based.*
> > meat from mammals, birds, fish and seafood, amphibians, insects, snails and grubs.
> > animal derived products; oils, eggs, roe, milk, cheese, yoghurt, honey
>
> *fungi based.*
> > mushrooms, both the fruit and the mycelia

A ***mixed diet*** includes components from each source. Analysis of our anatomy, particularly our teeth and our digestive system, shows that we evolved to be omnivores, eating a mixed diet. (But we are also very adaptable and can also survive on a vegetarian diet).

The Happiness Tree

B6.2.2 The Three Major Components
Our food includes three major components *Carbohydrates, Protein, and Fat* (plus important additional nutrients and structural material).

Any of the three components can be used (in different ways) by our bodies to provide energy (calories). However, we need *all three* components to grow and maintain our body and remain healthy. The three different food sources (plant, animal and fungi) contain varying amounts of these three components as shown in Figure B6.2. (Note that Figure B6.2 was copied from a diet book that the author cannot at present find the reference to).

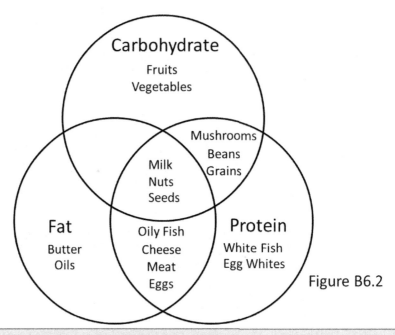

Figure B6.2

This shows the composition of common food sources in terms of the three major components, Carbohydrate, Fat and Protein. For instance, Egg Whites are all Protein, but Nuts contain Carbohydrate, Fat and Protein

You will see from Figure B6.2 above that some foods such as egg whites contain only one food component, protein. Others such as meat contain both protein and fat. Mushrooms and beans contain both carbohydrates and protein. Relatively few sources (milk, nuts, seeds) contain all three components, so there is benefit in a *mixed diet* as previously represented in Figure B6.1.

B6.2.3 Nutrient and Structural components
As well as Fat, Protein and Carbohydrates, our bodies need to obtain a wide range of additional nutrients from our food. These are summarised below.
- We need *vitamins*; these are essential and since our body does not manufacture all of them, it is essential that we get them from our diet (for example vitamin C).
- We need minerals and can only get them from our food and drink.

The Happiness Tree

- We also need a wide range of *phytonutrients* (a variety of plant chemicals such as polyphenols and other antioxidants). Although not as essential as vitamins, they are important to our resilience and long-term health, (see section B7.1 *herbs*).
- A supply of *enzymes* is important because they help us break down and digest food.
- *Insoluble fibre* provides the structural element that helps the mechanics of our digestive system and bowels.
- *Soluble fibre* is needed as a prebiotic to feed the bugs in our microbiome (see below B6.4)

The three food sources provide these nutrients broadly as follows:

plant based
> most of the required range of vitamins and minerals, structural fibre (soluble and insoluble), enzymes, and phytonutrients

animal based
> meat provides vitamins B12, B3, iron, zinc, iodine, phosphorus
> fish provides Omega3 fatty acid, vitamin D, thianine, selenium and iodine.
> organs such as liver provide vitamins A, B2, B9
> bones and cartilage provide collagen
> dairy products are rich in vitamins and calcium

fungi
> mushrooms contain vitamins B2,B3, B9, B5 and D, as well as minerals phosphorus, selenium, copper, and potassium.
> Mushrooms also contain unique beneficial compounds not found in plants or meat.

This variation in nutritional content between food types is another reason why a *mixed diet* is a good idea. For example, *Vegetarians and Vegans*, who don't eat animal-based food, may need to boost their intake of some nutrients like vitamin B12, iodine, calcium and omega 3 because these are not plentiful in plant based food.

On the other hand, current science is indicating that we need as little as 10% protein in our diet compared to 75-80% carbohydrate and 10-15% fat, so we don't need to eat a lot of meat, we can choose to have a diet that is mostly plant based.

B6.2.4 Some Unhealthy Food Sources

Here's a list of the foods that current research (TS and many others) suggests are bad for us. You will see that they are mostly foods that have been modified from their natural form:

Refined Sugar and Refined Carbs. The evidence for the unhealthy effects of consuming refined sugar is so great that some people have suggested we regard it as a drug. It's added to sweets, cakes, biscuits and fizzy drinks and most processed foods. It's even in supposedly healthy foods like cereals and fruit juices. Sugar is best avoided or at least eaten sparingly. Carbohydrates are rich in calories/energy but are better consumed from unrefined sources like whole grains and beans. (Much of the fibre and some of the nutrition lies in the skin or bran of grains and this is discarded to make white flour, rice or pasta. In Asia the transition from brown to white rice triggered an increase in a disease called Beri Beri).

Bad Fats and Oils. We need fats/oils in our diet. The low fat diet has been discredited, but there are good fats and bad fats. (see *"Fats That Kill and Fats That Heal"* by *Udo Erasmus*).

The fats that are widely considered most harmful are called **trans fats** or *hydrogenated fats*. They are chemically processed, usually from vegetable oils, to solidify them into products such as margarine.

Animal fats (lard, butter, cheese), fall largely into the category of *saturated fats.* These have for many years been considered bad for us and this idea triggered the trend to low fat diets, a shift to polyunsaturated fats such as vegetable oils, and to the more harmful trans fats. According to TS the bad reputation for animal fats may be an oversimplification because some people thrive on traditional diets that are high in animal fat.

There are also many **good fats**. There is strong evidence that olive oil (rich in monounsaturated fat) is very good for us, as is the essential fatty acid omega 3 (fish oil) and also omega 6 (seed oils). Some nut oils contain a mixture of oil types and are generally considered beneficial. (there may not yet be total consensus on the question of omega 3 and the balance with omega 6, but the recommendation to eat oily fish seems unanimous).

Artificial Additives and Preservatives This includes salt, sweeteners such as aspartame, flavourings such as MSG, other preservatives and colourants. They are all suspected of having negative effects.

Processed foods. In the last 50 years or so there's been a massive increase in the consumption of factory-made and chemically processed food. That includes anything that didn't grow, or anything that's been modified, for example bacon, sausages, burgers, kebabs, bread, pastries, cakes, pickles, smoked food, most salted, or cured foods etc. These foods are often based on only a few ingredients such as refined carbohydrates (white flour), trans fats (the worst kind of fat) and sugar (often corn syrup), so they lack the diversity that we (and our microbiome) need to thrive on. They are usually high in sodium and preservatives and low in nutrients and fibre.

(Note that there are a few lightly processed foods that are valuable.

- Fermented foods are good for us because they are probiotic.
- Frozen foods are generally good because they are frozen when very fresh and the process doesn't destroy many of the nutrients, additives are not needed, and we can still recognise what we're eating.
- Dried fruit and beans and peas.

- Some tinned foods vegetables and fish are relatively beneficial provided there aren't too many flavourings added.
- Food extracts such as oils are valuable especially if cold pressed.
- Vegetable juices are beneficial provided they don't contain preservatives or flavouring.)

"Recent" foods. Some people believe that wheat-based products, and dairy products may be bad for us, because we didn't start eating them until farming emerged around 10,000 years ago, and evolutionary changes to adapt to them were thought to be slow to occur. This view is supported by the fact that a small number of people are very allergic to the gluten in wheat (Coeliac disease) and some people are intolerant to milk (lactose intolerance). It has been further supported by the argument that in regions where dairy is not part of the diet, incidence of some types of disease is lower. It is also argued that dairy cows have been so selectively bred (to increase milk yield) that their milk contains an unnaturally high level of hormones.

However, according to *TS* the classification of wheat and dairy as unhealthy foods is a misleading oversimplification of a very complex subject. He also points out that it is now thought that some genetic adaptations to food can occur much more quickly than previously thought (aided by the actions of our microbiome).

The author has formed the personal view that in the face of this varied and conflicting advice, and in view of the nutritional value of grain and dairy based products, a sensible approach might be to

- notice if you have any adverse reactions to them and if not then continue to eat grains, but go for wholemeal rather than refined, and include a variety of grains rather than just wheat.
- continue to eat dairy in moderation but prefer fermented versions such as kefir and cheeses, especially unpasteurized goats' cheese and other cheeses that are rich in probiotic bacteria (avoiding processed cheese).
- If you choose to use soy based products as an alternative be aware that there are some health concerns about excessive consumption of soya based products (TS).

B 6.3 The Microbiome (The Good Bugs Inside Us)

B6.3.1 About the Microbiome

Research is increasingly pointing out the importance of our gut bacteria to our physical and mental health. We tend to think of bacteria as bad things and go to great lengths to keep our homes and bodies bug free. So, it may be a shock to find that each of us has a few kilograms of bugs living inside us in our intestines and bowels. We have about as many bug cells and bug DNA as we do human ones. We always have had, right through our evolution. We have evolved a symbiotic relationship with them, we host and feed them, and they perform essential biochemical tasks for us. They are like a biochemical factory inside us.

We can't live without them. They get passed on from mother to infant at birth and through breast feeding. These bugs perform numerous functions, including:

- the good bugs keep the bad ones (like salmonella, ecoli and c.difficile) in check so we don't as easily get food poisoning.
- they are an essential part of our digestive system
- they create numerous chemical compounds such as *neurotransmitters* for our brain (including serotonin, one of the *feel-good* chemicals)
- they generate the *melatonin t*hat helps us sleep
- they form a major part of our immune system.

These bugs keep us healthy. We need both a sufficient variety and quantity. If we are deficient in these good bugs, then we are more likely to get physically or mentally ill. We can be deficient from birth. This has been linked to caesarean section delivery and to feeding artificial milk. Or we may have 'inherited' a poor spectrum of bugs from our mother. We can also be deficient through having a poor diet (these good bugs don't thrive on junk food), or through intensive use of antibiotics that kill them.

Chris Woollams has written a book called *"Heal Your Gut Heal Your Body"*. It explains some of the recent research into the effects of gut bacteria on our health. It claims that inadequate gut bacteria may even be linked to a wide range of autoimmune diseases and many other things like cancer, depression, autism, and dyslexia. He explains that there is a lot of research going on into this subject and recommends that we boost our gut bacteria by diet or by supplements. Since his book was published the pace of research and public awareness has increased, it now attracts a lot of media attention (including the use of poo transplants) as more and more surprising results are discovered. Prof Tim Spector whose book we referred to earlier also stresses the importance of the microbiome and indicates that there also *epigenetic* factors at work. He is an expert on the subject, leading the largest microbiome research project in the UK. You can expect to hear more on this subject.

B6.3.2 How You Can Boost Your Microbiome

a) Eat probiotic foods. Many of our modern foods are pasteurised and contain no bugs. But there are several types of fermented foods that are rich in beneficial bacteria. They originated mostly in Asia or Central Europe and include *kefir,* which is a fermented milk and *kambucha,* which is a fermented tea. Other probiotic foods include *kimchi* and *sauerkraut.* Some Japanese fermented soya foods like *miso, tempeh,* and *netto* are also probiotic, as are some *olives. Raw goats' cheese* is also a probiotic (and an important part of the healthy Mediterranean diet). These fermented foods are increasingly available in the west but must be bought raw/unpasteurised. Fortunately, some stores are now selling them raw. Some can be made cheaply and easily at home, especially kefir. Alternatively, if you don't fancy fermented foods take a good quality probiotic supplement.

b) Eat prebiotic foods. These are not bugs, but are food for the good bugs, and pass undigested through the acid of the stomach to the gut. The idea is that if you feed this to the good bugs they will multiply and kill off the bad ones and give you a better population. Some prebiotic foods include oats and oat bran, wheat bran, rice bran, onions, leeks, garlic, dandelion leaves, chicory, globe artichokes, apple cider vinegar, apples, pectin and many more. You can also buy supplements such as inuline (extract from chicory). By eating a wide variety of vegetables and fruit you give your bugs a wider variety of prebiotic food and get a healthier more diverse range of bugs.

Note that it's a good idea to eat *both* probiotic and prebiotic foods to *maintain* a healthy microbiome. There is emerging interest in a third category called *postbiotics* which are the waste product of our microbes.

B6.4 Food and Mood

Scientists have identified various chemical compounds called neurotransmitters that play key roles in our brain function. They affect among other things our mood. These compounds are manufactured by our body from the food we eat. They include *serotonin, catecholamines (dopamine and adrenaline), GABA, endorphins and oxytocin*. They are sometimes referred to as the *feel-good* hormones. If, for whatever reason, our brain lacks sufficient of these compounds, then we can become unhappy, our mood drops, we can become depressed, and also may get cravings for some foods or drink. Since these important chemicals are made from our food, it seems to be a reasonable question to ask whether what we eat could also affect our brain chemistry and hence our mood. Some sources indicate that it can, and this leads to very *important additional implications* regarding our diet, as we shall see below.

Julia Ross MA is a psychotherapist who started practise in 1975 and is also a best selling author. In her second book The Mood Cure, she describes how she began to suspect that poor nutrition was a factor that might be affecting the low mood of some of her clients. In the 1980's she was motivated by the work of neuroscientist Kenneth Blum PhD who was working at the University of North Texas (see Journal of Psychoactive Drugs 1990 Apr-Jun;22(2). He was exploring the brain chemistry of alcoholics and drug addicts, and discovered genes that could hardwire the brain to underproduce the *feel good* hormones. He achieved some dramatic improvements by giving nutritional supplements to some patients. The supplements seemed to be able to override the genetic disposition of the patients to low mood and addiction. This inspired Julia Ross to explore a combination of nutritional therapy with psychotherapy, which she started doing in her California clinic and reports a high degree of success spanning more than 15 years. There are now clinics in the UK also practicing what is sometimes called *neuronutrition* therapy. The details are beyond the scope of this book but a few points are summarised here because they are directly relevant to diet.

According to her book a deficiency in serotonin, catecholamines, GABA or endorphins can produce low mood and changes in behaviour (craving, depression, anger etc.). The exact response is different for each hormone. She reports that the deficiencies can be caused by stress, by genes, by lack of exercise or sunlight, but also by **dietary deficiency**. In particular she states that these important brain chemicals are made from particular amino acids that are only present in protein and fats in large quantity. For that reason she recommends we eat plenty of meat, oily fish, dairy and eggs, including the previously discredited saturated fats such as butter, and particularly recommends full fat cottage cheese. She also states that we need a full range of vitamins in order to convert the amino acids to neurotransmitters (reinforcing the need for lots of fruit and veg) and that Vit D in particular has an important role in elevating mood. Goodbye low fat diet and welcome back sunshine!

In her clinic Julia Ross assessed her clients' particular needs and administered appropriate dietary supplements selected from a range including *5HTP, Tryptophan, SAMe, St John's Wort, Tyrosine, Omega 3* and *DLPA*.

Bear in mind that this is a complex topic so it's hard to be certain of all the conclusions. We are all different, what works for some may not work for others. It is also the case that the beneficial nutrients that we eat must be absorbed and distributed in sufficient quantity. They must cross the *gut/blood barrier* and the *blood/brain barrier* and so some food supplements may not be as effective in practice as they might appear in principle from just their nutrition content.

If you have mood problems, the author does not recommend that you try treating yourself with these supplements, rather consult a specialist. On the other hand, it seems well worth taking note of the dietary implications highlighted above and ensuring that you have adequate nutrition sunshine, and exercise to maintain a healthy level of neurotransmitters.

B 6.5 The Basics of Healthy Eating

The author has put together a summary guide for his own use, using the current science-based advice previously described. The guide list (below) isn't a diet as such, but rather a broad recommendation to eat mostly a mixed and wide range of natural and unrefined foods. It is not very restrictive: most of the traditional cuisines across the world can be created using the ingredients on this list. You can also easily adapt them to suit yourself. You can innovate and concoct an infinite number of healthy sweets, treats, snacks and meals.

Summary guide

- Avoid consuming the unhealthy and processed foods listed in 6.2.4 above, or at least limit your consumption to occasional "treats".
- Eat a mixed diet that includes plant-based foods (fruit, vegetables ,nuts, seeds), mushrooms, and animal-based products (meat, fish, dairy, eggs).
- Make the animal-based products the smaller part of your diet, eat mostly plant and mushroom based foods.
- Eat a wide variety of vegetables, fruit, berries, nuts, seeds, beans, whole grains and mushrooms and a wide variety of colours, because that way you (and your gut bacteria) get a wide variety of nutrients. Eat them with the skins on where possible (because that's where many of the nutrients and much of the fibre are located).
- Get your protein from eggs, oily fish, seafood, lean meat (especially white meat), mushrooms, beans, nuts and grains like quinoa.

- Use only healthy oils (e.g. olive oil, some nut oils) for salads and cooking, and make sure you get enough fish oil.
- Limit dairy intake if it disagrees with you. Also prefer fermented versions such as kefir and cheese, especially unpasteurized goats' cheese and other non pasteurised cheeses that are rich in probiotic bacteria (avoiding *processed* cheese).
- Limit wheat intake if it disagrees with you Use only whole grains (brown bread, brown rice etc), and include a range of other whole grains for variety (oats, rye, barley, quinoa, buckwheat, millet).
- Make beans and peas a significant part of your diet (fresh, dried, frozen, tinned).
- Eat some food raw (for the beneficial enzymes that are destroyed by cooking), for example salad, raw vegetables, fruit, berries, smoothies, vegetable juices, sprouted seeds, microgreens.
- Don't cook at high temperature or eat burned blackened food, prefer steamed or boiled to roasted or fried or barbecued.
- Use plenty of herbs and spices because they are beneficial as well as tasty: For example, chili, turmeric, ginger, garlic, basil, pepper and cinnamon. Treat yourself to the many tasty healthy options they help provide.
- If you need a sweet treat, use honey; its still a sugar but has some additional nutrients.
- Ensure you get enough fibre (eating vegetables helps here) both soluble and insoluble.
- Eat probiotic and prebiotic food.
- Drink adequate fluid to stay hydrated.
- Restrict your intake of sugary fruit juice and fizzy drinks, and limit alcohol consumption. (the official guidance in the UK *nhs.uk>better health* is currently to drink no more than 14 points a week spread across 3 days or more, because this limits risk of harming your health (that's 6 medium sized glasses of wine 175 ml or 6 pints of 4% beer)).

B6.6 How to Improve Your Diet.

Were all different. You may think a balanced diet is a burger in each hand, or you may think that these suggestions for eating healthily are crazy and see no reason to change. It's up to you. You may like your burger and chips, bacon sandwiches, cola drinks, cakes, and cookies so much that you think you couldn't change even if you wanted to. After all, evolution has hard wired us with cravings for sugar, carbs, and fat to aid survival when food was scarce. Also, it has equipped us with an instinctive reluctance to eat things we haven't eaten before. The author, (who is not fond of shopping or cooking) made a personal decision to try and eat more healthily, and found that it's not all bad news:

The **good news** is that despite the obstacles, you can make the switch and enjoy the benefits. A good way to start is to learn more about food (B6.2), so that you understand and believe in what you're attempting, as well as becoming aware of some of the treats awaiting you.

There's more **good news** that might encourage you:

- Healthy food is as delicious as unhealthy food and not difficult to prepare.
- Healthy unprocessed foods are increasingly available in our supermarkets
- Healthy foods are affordable and there's a huge variety.
- Tasty spices and herbs are good for us.
- Healthy food will help to stop you from getting seriously overweight. You can eat as much as you like of some of them.
- It doesn't take long to get to like new food, you just need to be willing to try it and acquire the taste.

There are many recipes and suggestions for healthy meals in magazines books and on the Internet. There are also *slimming groups* that help you learn about various aspects of healthier eating (the author has noticed that one at least of these groups promotes weight loss by healthy eating rather than by restrictive dieting).

If you're not sure where to start, just try one healthy meal that you think you might like and see how you get on. One small step leads to another. Even a partial switch will bring benefits, you don't have to rigidly follow a set of strict rules, and the odd relapse doesn't matter.

If you're very busy or you don't know how to cook this needn't be an obstacle. Grazing on some raw food, like nuts, raisins, salad and fruit, is easy and saves time. Frozen berries and vegetables can make a very convenient and tasty addition to your diet, and vegetable juices give you lots of nutrition in a small glass. Not peeling your fruit and vegetables saves time and boosts the nutrition content.

With a bit of ingenuity, you can make use of delicious food *combinations* that are highly nutritious and very easy to make. For example, use a blender to make smoothies using a variety of vegetables and fruits. Add some seeds, or kefir, or vegetable juice, or even some natural food extract powders.

You can also buy many foods *already combined* such as mixed fruit and nuts, mixed seeds, mixed herbs, blended spices, mixed salad, mixed vegetables, and tins of mixed beans. This makes it easier to get the variety you need with less effort. The possibilities are endless.

As a bonus some treats are healthy. Red wine has long been held to have health benefits. More recently, it seems that there is now compelling evidence (TS) that the phytonutrient flavonoid in the cocoa bean is highly beneficial to us and our microbiome, so chocolate is good for us though for maximum benefit you need to adjust to eating dark chocolate (70%). It is also said to be good for our mood (healthline.com).

If you have a particular health problem or think you are deficient in particular vitamins, then, if you learn a little bit about food nutrition you could make specific dishes to "boost" your diet and your health. There is a wealth of information to help you (for example books such as *Food Your Miracle Medicine by Jean Carper*). Some books have been written by authors who had personal health problems, and who helped resolve them (in part at least) by changing to a more natural diet. An example is *Emily Jane's* recipe book *Back to Natural Eating.*The writings of Hippocrates 300 BC (author of the Hippocratic Oath) show that diet, herbs, and lifestyle issues were at the heart of his medicine. (*D Cardenas 2013* referred to in *drgoodfood.org>news17 Jul 2018*).

B7 Choose to Get Adequate Rest

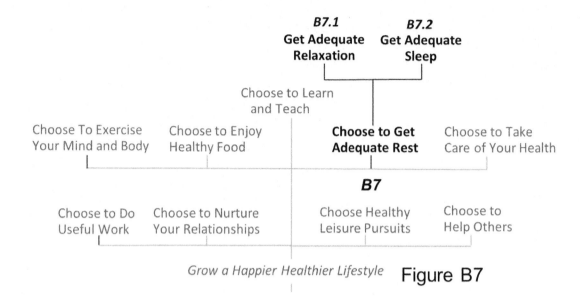

Figure B7

B7.1 Get Adequate Relaxation

B7.1.1 The Stress Response

Perceived stress signals automatically cause our brain to switch on a **"stress response"**, which puts us into a superhuman mode; our blood gets a surge of adrenaline, our pulse quickens, we get stronger and our brain speeds up. Our brainwave activity gets stronger and of higher frequency, we are then ready for **fight or flight**. This response helped us survive danger for a million years, but in modern life it can be a problem. That's because although we don't confront many tigers anymore, it seems that modern life nonetheless causes us to trigger the stress response very often. Scientists are gradually discovering how prolonged stress damages our health, not just by exhaustion, but for example by damaging our immune system. The list of serious illnesses attributable to stress is growing longer as research continues to focus on this problem.

Prolonged working, too much analytic thinking or trying to solve complex problems, worrying, interpersonal conflicts, can all lead to stress and nervous exhaustion. We need to take regular breaks to relax and give our mind a rest.

B7.1.2 The Relaxation Response

The *"relaxation response"* was first discovered by *Herbert Benson*. Just as our brain reacts to certain threat external cues to trigger a stress response, so it can respond to various cues from our body to trigger the opposite *relaxation response*. This causes several psychological and physiological changes to occur. For example it causes our brain to issue instructions to stop the generation of cortisol and adrenaline and instead release into the blood stream a range of healing and repair chemicals. It reduces our heart rate and can change the nature of our heart waveform. The relaxation response is also associated with a drop in the frequency of our electrical brainwaves from above 14 cycles per second (Beta) down to around 7 cps (Alpha). When we are in the relaxed mode our mind-body has the chance to repair and refresh itself.

The relaxation response is thought to be triggered by the action of the parasympathetic nervous system, particularly the vagus nerve, which connects the brain with many different parts of the body (think vagabond, it wanders everywhere).

We need to spend adequate time in a relaxed state. Some methods are listed below. There are many more. It's a good idea to experiment and find what works for you. There is a strong evidence base for the effectiveness and benefits of these relaxation techniques; see for example *L. Toussaint et al 2021 ncbi.nih.gov,* and *Lehrer.P.M and Woolfolk.R.L. Principles and Practice of Stress Management 2021 Guildford Press NY.*

Slow Deep Breathing triggers the relaxation response, probably by the action of the vagus nerve responding to pressure fluctuations on the heart caused by the breath. Such slow steady breathing causes the heart rate to vary up and down in time with the breathing (HRV). This is thought to trigger a signal via the vagus nerve to the brain which triggers the relaxation response. There are other techniques for stimulating the vagus nerve in various parts of the body.

The Relaxation Body Scan (also called PMR progressive muscle relaxation) is a process where you get comfortable , slow your breathing then concentrate your attention on each part of your body from head to toe, first creating tension in each selected muscle, then relaxing it so your whole body is progressively relaxed.(NB this is different from the Mindfulness body scan).

Massage can be helpful since it reduces muscle tension.

Visualisation for example using a Guided Relaxation CD is another a way of calming your body and your mind. Some CD's talk you through a body scan, encourage you to slow your breathing, then use words and music to encourage you to visualise relaxing situations.

Autogenics is a form of mental exercise involving autosuggestion to promote relaxation

Meditation and Mindfulness techniques produce relaxation, though this is not their primary function.

Biofeedback technology can be very effective and affordable, it's worth looking to see what's available. Some devices measure skin temperature and some your pulse. Some work on mobile apps and give onscreen visual cues to slow your breathing and display the resulting heart rate variability (HRV) that this produces.

AVS audio visual stimulation. This involves synchronised stimulation with light and sound at a particular repetition rate, using LED glasses and earphones. The flicker rate starts high at 14 cps or more (beta), then gradually drops to 7 cps or less (alpha). By gradually dropping the frequency of the stimulation the brain itself drops its brainwave frequency (through a mechanism called entrainment) into the relaxed alpha range or lower. This effect has been researched for many years using Electroencelograph (EECG) to measure brainwave frequency changes. It has been proven to lower the brainwave frequency, promote relaxation and sleep. It's not suitable for anyone prone to having fits. *(NYJ Tang et al 2014 ncbi.nlm.nih.gov, Yi-Yeh et al 5 july 2022 researchgate.net>3515)*

Music can help us relax and has many other beneficial effects on our mind (Prof Michael Spitzer bigthink.com)

Virtual Reality (VR) headsets are also being used as a mean of relaxation as well as enhancing meditation.

B7.2 Get Adequate Sleep

B7.2.1 The Importance of Sleep

During sleep many important processes occur in our mind/body. Adequate good quality sleep is essential to our health and wellbeing. Without it we soon deteriorate both physically and mentally. Without good sleep we lack concentration and can't see things clearly. We become accident prone and a hazard to others (e.g. if driving). Sleep deprivation has even been used as a form of torture. Jet lag seems to have a similar effect to sleep deprivation.

We are all different, some people seem to need more sleep than others, some are deep sleepers and some light sleepers. Some people suffer from insomnia, and have great difficulty getting enough sleep, others can fall asleep at the drop of a hat. Most of us have more difficulty sleeping if we are tense and have "something on our mind". It's not just quantity of sleep that's important but also quality. You should wake up feeling refreshed.

B7.2.2 Sunshine and Our Body Clock

We have a body clock (*ninds.nih.gov>brain-basics*) which includes two internal biological mechanisms; circadian rhythm and homeostasis These work together using a range of cues (such as light or darkness) to direct a wide range of functions and regulate our sleep cycle. One mechanism is by regulating our levels of *melatonin*, a hormone that induces us to sleep, and *serotonin* which makes us active and awake. One of the ways that this body clock is synchronised is by sunlight. A particular blue colour that's present in sunlight is detected by a sensor in our eyes. If this blue light is present, the sensor sends a message to the brain signalling the need to generate serotonin.

Those of us who live in northern or southern climes or cloudy climates may not get much sun in winter, so our serotonin levels may drop inducing what has been termed seasonal affective disorder SAD, especially if our lifestyle or the climate results in us staying indoors for long periods. Some people counter this by using "daylight" or "white" lightbulbs that emit a spectrum that includes the required blue colour. If you've chosen " daylight " bulbs in your house, you may need to switch them off in the evening and use instead bulbs that lack the blue colour. They will appear slightly more orange or red. Red lighting in the evening seems to feel more relaxing.

There's another potential problem. Many of our computer screens, TVs and phones emit this same colour of blue, so if you use them late at night you may have trouble sleeping through lack of melatonin. You can buy screen filters, and some screens have options to reduce blue light.

B7.2.3 Our Sleep Cycle

We have a *sleep cycle*, (*my.clevelandclinic.org>health*) and as we go through the cycle our brain wave frequency (cycles per second or cps) changes. We start awake (*beta* brainwaves 14-32 cps), then relaxed (*alpha* waves 7-14 cps), then half asleep (*theta* 4.5-7 cps) then into deep dreamless sleep (*Delta* 0.5-4 cps). Later in the night we go into a different sleep mode called REM where our eyes move rapidly, and we dream (*theta, alpha, beta)*. At the end of the cycle, (at around 90 minutes) we come back to half awake (*theta*) then fully awake (*beta*). We may repeat this cycle several times in one night. Frequent interruptions to this natural cycle might disrupt the quality of our sleep.

B7.2.4 Tips on Sleeping

Many of us suffer from insomnia or poor-quality sleep. Here are a few tips you might want to try. There's a wealth of further information and advice available online.

Avoid caffeine in the latter part of the day, and get some exercise so that you are physically tired in the evening. Avoid sleeping in the day.

A good way to initially get to sleep is to do some form of *relaxation* exercise first. This helps to relax your body, release muscle tension, and calms your mind (getting it into the *alpha* state). Any of the methods described earlier in B7.1 for relaxation will help you get to sleep.

Persistent thoughts or worries can be a particular obstacle to sleep. A period of meditation before sleep can help calm the mind and prepare it for sleep.

Some people find counting works. There are many variations such as counting backwards from a hundred. Counting helps keep out unwanted thoughts that would otherwise keep us awake.

Another good idea is to deliberately slow your breathing down. Also maybe count as you breathe in slowly and count again as you breath out.

Many find reading a book helps them go to sleep.

Herbal supplements or teas might help, some popular ones are chamomile, valerian, hops, passionflower, ginseng or you can supplement melatonin or GABA.

Some find that aromatherapy helps (some popular essential oils include lavender, chamomile, valerian, geranium and many more). They can be vapourised or diluted with a carrier or sprayed on your pillow (you need to be cautious and learn how to use them because they can irritate).

Eating makes us feel drowsy but eating a heavy meal shortly before bedtime seems to lead to poorer quality sleep (this may be because our microbiome needs to be busy making essential chemicals during sleep). Similarly, alcohol helps us relax and drop off more easily but can have a negative effect later during the REM phase (as well as making it more likely that we will have to get up during the night).

Some people believe it's best to sleep in a dark room with no phones or electrical equipment on (no EMF's) and to be woken by gradually increasing light, thus mimicking our natural environment. (Its not clear if there is evidence to support this and at present there is disagreement among scientists as to whether EMF's are a hazard). Adequate ventilation is a good idea, and not too high a temperature. It's important to have a comfortable mattress, it's worth finding out what suits you best.

If you suffer from chronic insomnia, the AVS devices mentioned earlier have been found by some to be very effective, and there is evidence to back this up from trials on subjects who had difficulty sleeping because of pain. (HY Tang 2019 journals.sagepub.com>abs).

Some smart watches monitor your sleep pattern. You can also buy EECG devices for home use that work with your mobile to monitor your sleep pattern.

Whatever solutions you adopt, it is thought by many that establishing a routine or pattern helps you get better sleep. This means for example going to bed at a regular time each night, after spending a period of time with low lighting and screens off, doing something relaxing.

B7.2.5 Training to Sleep Anywhere Anytime

Some people such a soldiers and emergency workers need to be able to sleep *whenever* and *wherever* they can, even in noisy and uncomfortable environments. It seems that it's possible to train ourselves to do just that. One technique for doing this was first described in a *1981* book *Relax and Win, Championship Performance* by *Bud Winter.* The technique has recently been popularised in a *YouTube* video by *Justin Agustin* who says the technique is used by the US military. It is summarised below. You will see that it combines elements of slow breathing, relaxation, and visualization.

- Lie down and take some deep breaths
- Progressively relax the muscles in your forehead, then your cheeks then your jaws.
- Focus on your breathing
- Move your attention down to your neck and shoulders, ensure they aren't tensed up, drop your shoulders as low as you can, keeping your arms and hands by your side.
- Imagine a warm sensation going from your head to your fingertips, then from your heart to your toes.
- Take a deep breath and as you exhale focus on relaxing your stomach, then on down to your thighs, knees, legs, feet, relaxing each area in turn.
- Calm and clear your mind by imagining that you are lying in a canoe on a calm lake with nothing but a clear blue sky above....or ..that you are lying in a black velvet hammock in a pitch black room.
- If you are still distracted by thoughts, repeat to yourself for 10 seconds "don't think, don't think, don't think"

The author has not tried this, but it is claimed that if you train yourself to do this every night for 6 weeks then you will be able to fall asleep anytime, anywhere, within 2 minutes.

B8 Choose to Protect Your Health

Caveat . If you have a health problem consult your health professional. If you want to try any of the things suggested here, check it out with your health professional first.

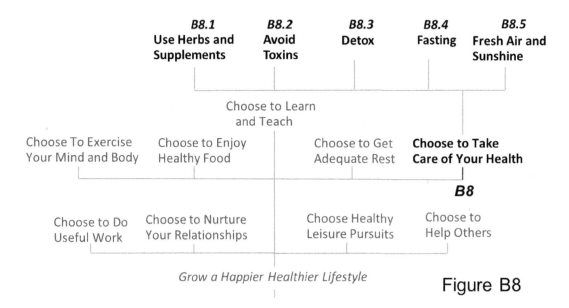

Figure B8

B8.1 Use Herbs and Supplements

B8.1.1 Background

Many people now use *herbs* and other *dietary supplements* such as vitamins and minerals to boost their health, counter a particular ailment, or achieve a particular objective such as better sleep. They are also used by many as a preventive measure with the aim of protecting and maintaining their long-term health. The term *vitamin loyalty* is sometimes used to refer to this phenomenon. It has been estimated that about 1/3 of the UK population take supplements, making it a very large business. Is it worth it? Are they wasting their money? Is there evidence that they work?

There are conflicting viewpoints on the answers to these questions and on the subject in general. It very contentious. You've probably heard your Doctor or health professional say that *"you get all the vitamins you need from a balanced diet"*. Probably true, but what about the millions of us who don't have a healthy diet?

Doctors have a very justifiable concern that patients may self-diagnose or harm themselves by taking inappropriate supplements or over large doses or that they might take supplements that interfere with a prescribed medication. There are also concerns about lack of regulation and quality control.

The public on the other hand may feel tempted to try some supplements because they believe that they will have fewer side effects than many drugs. Also people are reluctant to overload the health service by consulting a professional about minor ailments that they feel they can treat themselves.

We all must make our own minds up about this subject. In this section the author briefly examines the subject in search of any useful indicators that might help us decide. We will address herbs separately from other supplements such as vitamins and minerals.

B8.1.2 Herbs
What are they?

The term *herb* generally means a part or extract of a plant form that has medicinal or culinary benefits. This can include the leaves, roots, bark, skin, fruit, seeds, nuts, flowers, oils and other extracts of a wide range of plants, vegetables, bushes, and trees. It also includes mushrooms. (The author likes to think of herbs as fruit and veg that happen to contain a particularly high level of phytonutrients).

Herbs are available in many forms; fresh whole, dried, chopped or powdered. They are also available as capsules, tablets, teabags, oils, tinctures, and various other forms of extracts.

Some History

Herbal medicine has been around for many thousands of years. Our early ancestors evolved eating wild plants, fruits and vegetables and gradually learned which ones had medicinal properties. This practical knowledge was passed on orally then later, in written form. For thousands of years herbal medicine was mainstream medicine, it was all we had. In many parts of the world, it still is. Some traditional forms of Asian medicine such as the Indian Ayurvedic system and the Chinese Traditional Medicine (TCM) both use herbs extensively and are in widespread use today. In China it is normal for a medical doctor to qualify in both TCM and modern medicine, and to practise both forms together. In China some specific TCM herbs were officially endorsed for use in the fight against Covid. In Thailand Andrographis Particulata was authorized for use in Covid hospitals following a local trial.

In early medieval Britain *monks* kept herb gardens and administered herbal medicine to the public. Later *apothecaries* took on a similar role. Only the rich could afford to consult Physicians, whose medical and herbal texts were written in Latin and not accessible to the public. In 1652, a Cambridge educated Physician and Botanist, *Dr Nicholas Culpeper*, published a groundbreaking book *"The English Physician"*, which was later called *"The Complete Herbal"*. Culpeper was notoriously scathing of the methods of his fellow physicians. He set himself the mission of translating herbal medical texts from Latin and using his knowledge and experience to produce a book that would bring *medicine to the masses*. His book was hugely successful and influential and is still in print today. It was particularly popular in the emerging North American Colonies (there is still a chain of "Culpeper Herb Stores" in Canada). He was arguably the first Doctor in the UK to make medicine available to the wider public.

It's worth noting that many herbs and natural remedies subsequently became the basis for a drug or commercial medicine. For example, willow bark extract became *aspirin*, cinchona tree bark extract became *quinine* (used to fight malaria). Foxglove was the precursor to *digitalis* and red clover to *warfarin*. There is ongoing interest in developing novel drugs from herbs (LT Lin, 2014 ncbi.nim.nih.gov>pmc).

Dr James Duke has published a bestselling book *The Green Pharmacy* that is an excellent modern overview of the use of herbs. He is a botanist specializing in the chemical make-up of plants. He spent 30 years working all over the world documenting and researching the composition of wild plants for the US Department of Agriculture. During that time, he interviewed thousands of traditional healers and scientists in remote regions. He created a unique database of the compounds found in plants, and the healing properties that healers attributed to them.

Are Herbs Beneficial?

All forms of plant life must defend themselves against the same types of attackers or threats that we do. These threats include viruses, bacteria, parasites, fungi, moulds, yeasts, oxidants, insects and UV from sunlight. Plant life has been around much longer than we have, and over a half billion or so years plants have involved some amazing, complex, and very effective defenses ((Fraenkel 1959, Walker 1994). Some of these are chemicals called *phytonutrients*. There are many sub classes including *polyphenols* which are powerful antioxidants. They are part of the plant's immune system; they can counter or kill specific threats. When we eat the plants, we gain the benefit of their defenses (livescience.com>5254). They act as powerful antioxidants and are anti-inflammatory. They may also enhance immunity and enhance intercellular communication, repair DNA damage from toxins, detoxify carcinogens and alter oestrogen metabolism.

Some of these *polyphenols* are concentrated at the plant interfaces with the air and the soil (because that's where the threat primarily comes from). This includes the outer surfaces of leaves, the skins of fruit and roots, the bark of stems or branches. Seeds and nuts also have to be well protected and so they too are often packed with phytonutrients (and other forms of nutrition).

Rather than rely on a single compound, plants have evolved a wide range of phytonutrients. These work together *synergistically* and so achieve a higher effectiveness, and we in turn can benefit from that *synergy* when we eat them. We also benefit from the fact that the compounds are organic not synthetic, because it often means that our bodies can more readily absorb them: they are said to be more *bioavailable*.

You may hear or read *that "there is no evidence to support the benefits claimed for this herb"*. This may be true, because no company is going to pay millions of dollars to fund trials on a herb which is readily available, cheap, and can't be patented. It's desirable for medicine to be evidence based, but it's not surprising to find that for many herbs and supplements, evidence in the form of reliable human trials results, is likely to remain limited for this economic reason.

There is however some evidence. The German Government in 1978 set up Commission E, a multidiscipline team to set up a process to affirm the effectiveness and safety of herbs (phytomedicines). They published 380 monographs on the use of herbs. These have been translated into English and presented in the American Botanical Council's *The Complete German Commission E Monographs, Therapeutic Guide to Herbal Medicine.* Consequently, herbal remedies are now widely prescribed by GPs in Germany and account for 10% of pharmaceutical sales (cherylherbs.com>blog). For example, since 1988 the herb *St John's Wort* (an ancient remedy for mental illness, and one notoriously cited as interacting with other medications) has been prescribed for depression. It outsells Prozac in Germany *(mcgill.ca>oss.article 30 may 2017)*.

The effects of herbal compounds such as phytonutrients and polyphenols are the subject of an increasing amount of scientific research. There is positive evidence emerging from test tube research and from animal trials. This evidence, albeit small scale, sometimes shows the detailed mechanisms by which herbs work. For illustration, some anti-viral herbs can block enzymes that a virus relies on to survive and function. Others can block the spike that the virus uses to penetrate a cell. Others can impair the virus's ability to reproduce within a cell. Such research doesn't give the same level of evidence as full- scale human trials, but it does give insight into the way herbs work and may also help development of novel medicines.

Herbs may not display the dramatic power or speed of some drugs (such as antibiotics). They are however generally perceived to have fewer negative side effects and to be *relatively* safe. In addition, they don't damage your microbiome as antibiotics can. Some herbs may be effective in cases where drugs are not effective, for example countering viruses.

You will make up your own mind. On balance the author personally has concluded that herbs are useful, even though there is not, and may never be, extensive full scale human trials evidence to support their use. This view is based on the facts that:

- the small-scale, test-tube evidence that exists is supportive
- the German Commission E initiative was positive
- herbal remedies are widely prescribed by GPs in Germany and account for 10% of pharmaceutical sales (cherylherbs.com>blog)
- there is a long and documented history of safe useage
- they are affordable, available, and generally safe and have few side effects
- if the official *5 a day fruit and veg* is good advice, then herbs are also likely to be beneficial, because both involve largely the same types of phytonutrients

Dr Duke advises that, if you want to use herbs, you must be careful. You must take a cautious approach because they are not risk free just because they are natural. He advises:

- Don't self-diagnose; consult a professional practitioner.
- Make sure you've got the genuine herb.
- Make sure you don't overdose,

- watch out for side effects or allergies.
- If you're on medication, consult your health practitioner to make sure the herb doesn't interact with it.
- If you are pregnant or very ill, be particularly careful to avoid anything that could harm you.

There is a wealth of information available for you to learn from, including many helpful websites such as *healthline.com.* and *canceractive.com.* and many helpful books.

B 8.1.2 Vitamin and Mineral Supplements

Here we are talking about vitamins and minerals in the form of *synthetic* nutrients as distinct from their *natural* counterparts found in food, food extracts and herbs. A sizeable percentage of Western populations take vitamin and mineral supplements, often a multi vitamin and mineral pill MVM, or individual pills such as Vitamin C, D and Zinc. The market in the US is variably reported as between $4Billion and over $10 Billion and growing.

Do we need them? There are thousands of articles and books telling us, in detail, how to use them and how well they work to support and optimize our health. Many nutritionists support their use and say that it's backed by science: (Patrick Holford *The Optimum Nutrition Bible,* the Editors of Rodale Press *Healing with Vitamins and Minerals,* The Readers Digest *Guide to Vitamins Minerals and Supplements,* Dr Richard Firshein *The Nutraceutical Revolution*). There are some scientific studies that support the use of some vitamins such as vitamin D.

But many other science-based sources indicate that there is little or no evidence to support the use of vitamins and minerals. (*TS the Diet Myth, Mary Brown Aug 17 2016 healthline.com,* and many others).

The official advice from the UK NHS (*nhs.uk>food-and-diet*) is that in general we get all the vitamins and minerals we need from a healthy and varied diet. It recommends only very limited use:

- Vit D3 if you can't get sunshine
- Vit A, C, D for young children
- Folate during pregnancy.

You must make your own mind up. From a personal viewpoint the author, who previously used multivitamins, was very surprised to find these contradictory views, and now concludes that there is insufficient evidence to support the general use of synthetic vitamins and supplements. He can't but help wondering if he has missed something or that there's a missing piece of the jigsaw needed to explain these unusually strong and contradictory views. Some suggest its due to a lack of incentive to conduct vitamin trials, others that we use vitamins to salve our conscience because we prefer to stick with an unhealthy diet? Another viewpoint sometimes expressed is that whilst we may be deficient in vitamins due to poor diet, we can't solve the problem by taking *synthetic* vitamins because our bodies don't absorb or use them as well as those from *natural* sources such as food, natural food extracts and herbs (whose nutrients are said to be more *bioavailable* and to work in combination *synergistically*). Instead of synthetic vitamins you could try food *boosting* as suggested above in B6.6.

Overall, the author has formed the opinion that the only *sure* way to protect your health is through eating a varied diet of natural foods and herbs (supplementing with food extracts if need be).

B8.2 Avoid Toxins.

Our bodies cope with a range of toxins, some of which our ancestors weren't subjected to. It's an idea to be aware of some of them and take steps to reduce unnecessary exposure. Our bodies have amazing defences, but there's little point in overloading them. Our governments are continually striving to make our environment, homes and lifestyles safer, and we are already alerted to the dangers of pollution, smoking, alcohol and substance abuse. In many ways our homes are safer than they used to be, and many toxic substances (eg creosote, asbestos) have already been banned. It's still a good idea to take precautions when dealing with materials such as weedkiller, wood preserver or other powerful household chemicals, and follow the directions on the label. (A well- known brand of weed killer is currently the subject of legal action over a claim that it causes cancer). Its sensible to avoid inhaling smoke and also dust from wood or masonry when doing DIY.

B8.2.1 Water

Most of us are lucky enough to have water that is safe to drink. If you haven't or you don't want to drink tap water that has traces of chlorine or fluoride in it then consider using a water filter. There are lots of options. Some have the benefit of adding trace minerals to the water.

B8.2.2 Food

If you aren't using organic, remember to wash your fruit and vegetables to remove traces of pesticide. Rinsing under a tap is better than soaking. Some people add baking soda or vinegar to a bowl of water and wash their vegetables in that. It's also a good idea to rinse beans and grains like rice, because they may have been dried in the sun by just laying them on the ground.

B8.2.3 Household and Personal Hygiene Products

We need to take sensible steps to keep our home clean and our food free from harmful bacteria like *e.coli, salmonella,*and *c.difficile*. Also no one wants to be thought smelly or dirty, and we want to protect our children from harmful bacteria. But we seem to be in danger of going too far and instead risk poisoning our homes and bodies with a vast range of chemicals in an attempt to make them sterile and pleasant smelling; (this is sometimes referred to by scientists as *hygiene hysteria*). Look in your cupboards; how many of those cans, bottles, sprays, powders and air fresheners do you really need? How do you know they aren't harmful? They certainly aren't natural. Manufacturers must test their products, but they can't easily test for long term effects. It's not practical to prove that a product won't cause you harm in twenty years' time.

Step back from the advertisements, reflect that we evolved in a world full of bacteria and they are part of us. It is not only pointless to try and create a sterile environment, but it is actually harmful, because being exposed to bacteria helps our children develop their immune system. Studies have shown that children brought up in farm environments, where they are exposed to a vast array of bacteria from dirt, and animals and bugs, develop stronger immune systems. They tend to have fewer infections and allergies later in life than do their city cousins who are brought up in more sterile environments. (When scientists started to explore this possibility, they called it the *Hygiene Hypothesis* and it has since been proven to be correct: *(TS, and npr.org>2012/03/23)).*

This may lead you to cut down on the number of products you buy, or to seek more natural or more safe alternatives. In doing so you will also be helping the planet since many of the chemicals end up as pollutants in the sea or the air.

B8.2.4 Mental Toxins

The media (TV, movies, videos, social media, websites, newspapers, magazines etc.) play a hugely valuable role in keeping us informed, educated, entertained and 'socially joined up'. Recent technologies have made this even more accessible and useful. The media can have a powerful positive influence on us; but it's not a bad idea to watch out for negative aspects that might arise if we get over exposed. A couple of examples are described below. These are just personal opinions; you may think entirely differently and be totally immune:

When we access some aspects of the media, we become subjected to a powerful influence to want more and to buy more. This is good for business and maybe for most people it *goes over their head* but for some it can become a negative influence by promoting envy, greed and materialism (as well as pollution). We can, especially children, be made to feel dissatisfied with what we've got, and with who we are. Some people therefore choose to limit their, or their children's, exposure.

Most people are keen to know what's going on in the world and want to keep up to date. Many people take great pleasure in reading their daily paper or watching the TV news or going online, and that's fine. The media do a great job in this respect. The author also likes to access the "News" but finds that, for him, it seems to be the case that more emphasis is often given to bad news than to good news, and so he chooses to limit his exposure or have a holiday from it sometimes.

He thinks of it this way;
> good news is not "News, "
> so all "News" is bad news
> so no "News" is good news.

Noise pollution for some can be extremely annoying, and it's hard to avoid; the author finds ear defenders handy on some occasions.

B 8.3 Detox

Our bodies are amazingly capable of eliminating toxins mainly through the action of our kidneys, liver, sweat glands, and lymphatic system. These all need adequate water to function, so it's very important that we drink enough water. How much we need may vary, depending on our size, lifestyle and the climate we live in. In the UK the official guidance from *nhs.uk>eat-well>water* recommends that we need 6-8 cups or glasses of fluid a day (that's 1.5-2.5 L). including water, sugar free drinks, tea and coffee. Another source *health.com* suggests 1/30 th of our weight in Kg; that's 2L if you weigh 60KG, and 3L if you weigh 90 Kg. The author previously thought, as some suggest, that we should just drink when we're thirsty, but after two incidents of problems due to dehydration he has changed his mind and is now more cautious. Its also the case that some drinks, like alcohol, can dehydrate us, so if we over-indulge we need extra water. There is currently not a quick and convenient scientific check for us to use (but fitness watch manufacturers may soon change that). There is advice to drink more if you notice that you aren't urinating enough, or if your urine is dark (rather than straw coloured). There is also a useful *pinch test* where you pinch the skin on the back of your hand or finger and see how quickly the resulting skin fold disappears. (*health.com>news>skin test, TikTok video by Dr Karan Raj*)

A healthy diet results in us ingesting fewer toxins in the form of additives, and some foods and herbs may also help our organs and lymph system to stay healthy and eliminate toxins. For instance, the herb *milk thistle* has been proven to help the liver combat toxins and the effects of alcohol (*pubmed.ncbi.nim.nih.gov N Polachi et al Eur J M Chem 2016, and healthline.com 19 jan 2018*).

There is now a popular view that in everyday life our bodies build up a high level of toxins that can impair our health, and that we need to regularly *detox*. This view is promoted widely by health advocates, in the media, and by the detox industry that has grown up around it. However, the promotional literature of many detox products does not refer to any evidence to support its claims. Some common detox methods are briefly described below:

Detox Regimes

There are many variations, some target organs such as the liver, because it plays a major role in eliminating toxins. They usually involve a regime that lasts from a few days to a few weeks. A common theme is to combine fasting with drinking only vegetable juice and water (all in themselves seen generally as healthy). One drastic liver detox involves drinking olive oil mixed with Epsom salt.

Commercial Detox Products

There is a vast range of drinks, detox waters, teas, pills and potions available, some of them herbal. There are also herbal supplements that help rid you of parasites, yeasts and fungi (that can otherwise play havoc with your health). There are also detox pads that you put on the soles of your feet. These are claimed to remove toxins while you sleep: (they are a traditional detox therapy, though in a brief search, the author found no obvious scientific evidence that they work: who knows? he plans to give it a try).

Sweating

Sweating is one of the body's mechanisms for removing toxins, so exercise and saunas are both claimed to help. There's a particular form of sauna that heats your body using *far infra-red* (*FIR*) from electrically heated carbon panels. This is claimed to be particularly effective because the rays can penetrate deeper into the body, and cause fat cells to release stored toxins that are then removed by the lymph system or by sweating. These are commercially available as portable units for home use. The promotional material usually doesn't cite any scientific evidence to support them, but there is some: Analysis of toxins in sweat has shown that such saunas can help eliminate heavy metal toxins such as *cadmium lead and mercury (M Sears et al ncbi.nim.nih.gov)* and *FIR* has been used to treat people seriously poisoned by these metals, because it is safer than the previously used method called *chelation*.

Saunas may have other benefits. A prior session of *FIR* is claimed to help you more readily stretch muscles. Medical studies have linked the regular use of traditional saunas with lower death rates from heart disease. (*ncbi.nim.nih.gov>pmc Laukkanen et al 27 jan 2021*). Some sources also suggest that by deliberately raising your body temperature (within safe limits) you simulate the effects of a fever (*hypothermia*), and that this helps kill some bacteria and viruses. FIR has even been used in some 'alternative' clinics as a cancer treatment. This topic of using heat to treat illness is under scientific investigation; (*ncbi.nim.nih.gov>pmc Turning up the heat on Covid, M Cohen 2020*).

Exercise

Lymph fluid flows through channels round our body and, among other things, it collects toxins from our tissues and lymph nodes and delivers them back to the liver and kidneys via the blood stream for disposal. This lymph fluid is not driven by a pump but relies on our physical movements (and the effect of one-way valves) to move it successfully round the system. This is one of the many reasons why exercise is important for our health. A particular form of exercise called *rebounding* (using a small trampoline fitted with a safety handle) is advocated by some as a particularly effective form of exercise for the lymph system. It is claimed that the up/down acceleration causes the lymph valves to open and close and so forces the lymph to flow round the system. This is claimed to benefit swollen legs (lymphoedema) as well as being a means of aiding detox. There's not much scientific evidence to support the claims but a *NASA* study done in 1980 is widely quoted as having shown that rebounding is a more efficient exercise than jogging. The study is quoted as indicating that rebounding produced more blood flow and higher oxygen consumption than running on a treadmill, and that 10 minutes rebounding is equal to 33 minutes jogging (the author hasn't seen the actual report). It's also low impact and claimed to improve balance among elderly people.

Some yoga and Qi Gong exercises, and also deep breathing exercises, are thought by some to aid detox, possibly by massaging internal organs and boosting blood and lymph circulation (and the *Qi*). Some forms of massage boost circulation, and so may help the body's mechanisms of eliminating toxins (as well as being relaxing).

Does Detox Work?

Despite widespread promotion of detox in general, and the vast range of products available, there appears to be not a great deal of scientific evidence presented that our bodies routinely need detoxing. Promotional material for products often does not present much evidence to support the claims that they remove toxins. On the other hand, as we have seen above, there is evidence that some work, and plausible arguments as to how they might help our body's own detox system to do it's job more effectively. Some of the practices described above also have additional, more general, health benefits. It seems to be a bit of *a mixed bag*. You will have to make your own mind up whether any of these detox methods are for you. When you read promotional material, it might be a good idea to look and see if there is any scientific evidence quoted.

B8.4 Fasting

Fasting has been practised for thousands of years. You may be unaware of it, or view it with scepticism, or think it's something that only weird people do. Recent research has produced some astonishing results. One type of fasting was shown to not only alleviate but cure patients with Type 2 Diabetes *(medicalnewstoday.com 29 Dec 2021)*. Recently it has been suggested that fasting before and during chemotherapy increased the effectiveness of chemo and reduced the side effects because fasting causes the body to switch off many cells, so they survive the treatment. Other studies indicate that fasting helps rebuild a depleted immune system. Fasting is also becoming popular for those wishing to lose weight. There are different variations such as

- Fasting by eating only once in any 24 hours, for many days in a row
- Fasting for one day
- Fasting for two days out of five regularly
- Fasting for several days
- Fasting where you allow yourself some minimal food especially juices

The science behind this is not yet mature, and there's not yet a consensus of opinion, but it's a subject of great interest currently so expect to hear more about how effective fasting is, or isn't, in the future.

B8.5 Get Fresh Air and Sunshine

We were designed by evolution for an outdoor life; we had to be out and about to hunt and gather. Nowadays many of us spend almost our entire life indoors. We benefit if we get out and about. Think of the sayings *"it was like a breath of fresh air"* .and *"was like a ray of sunshine"*

Here are some reasons why we benefit:

Serotonin is one of the neurotransmitters that makes us feel happy. Our brain is triggered to increase serotonin when our eyes detect a particular blue colour in sunlight. In winter, if you live in a cloudy part of the world and stay indoors too much you may not get enough sunlight. This leads to a form of depression called *seasonal affected disorder SAD*. The best solution is to get out in the sun when you can.

Indoor environments can be less than healthy. To keep our houses warm we may restrict ventilation. Synthetic materials and heating sources can give off toxins and fumes that build up in the air. Dust can be another negative factor. Humidity can become too high or too low, and in damp buildings mould can build up and release spores.

Apart from toxins our interior spaces tend to lack the negative ions that occur naturally outside. Negative ions are believed to have a positive effect on our brain and our mood, possibly by increasing the blood flow to the brain. (webmd.com>features Pierce 2 Jun 2003). Some places, like forests, mountains and near breaking waves or water, have higher concentrations of negative ions. Maybe that's why we're attracted to them. You can buy small negative ion generators to use indoors, they are claimed to be effective in combatting Seasonal Affective Disorder (M Terman et al Journal of Alternative and Complementary Medicine Vol 1 no 1 1995). They have the added benefit of decreasing the level of dust, spores and pollution in the air in the air. More recently they have aroused interest as a possible way of removing viruses. There are also some negative reports so if you chose to buy one, check it out first and make sure it does not produce ozone. There are no negative reports about the benefits of being outside in fresh clean air.

Many of us have been bombarded with instructions to *"cover up, stay out of the sun"*. This advice was well meant and intended to reduce the risk of skin cancer. But it is now thought to have been bad advice overall. Scientists and oncologists now say that if you stay out of the sun, you have a greater risk of other cancers (and other diseases such as rickets), and that this outweighs the risk of skin cancer. This is partly because the action of sunlight on our skin produces vitamin D which is essential to our health and is a potent anti- cancer agent. Vitamin D is also an important factor in resisting viral infection, and studies in 2020 indicated that patients with low vitamin D were more seriously affected by Covid19, though at the time this was contested (ncbi.nim.nih.gov>pmc D Ghelani et al.2021). Sunlight also reduces our blood pressure slightly. Sunlight contains far infra- red wavelengths. These penetrate deeper into the body and make us feel warm and relaxed.

So, we need sunlight. Many people are now vitamin D deficient because of staying indoors for too long, or totally blocking the sun with cream, or totally covering up. In addition, some sun creams are suspected of being bad for our health (as well as of polluting the environment). This includes those containing organic filters such as *oxybenzone*. (see *BBC.com/ health, What science says about ingredient safety,Jessica Brown July 2019)*.It may be safer to use an inorganic *mineral based* sunscreen (which our body does not absorb).

You will find considerable variation in the available advice on sun exposure, cancer, health, sun cream and Vitamin D, and quite a few contradictory viewpoints. The certainties seem to be that:

- Too much sun exposure causes skin cancer, as well as damaging your skin
- Sun creams help prevent skin cancer (but choose a safe one)
- Some sun exposure is good for us and we need it to produce Vit D

The NHS website *england.nhs.uk>skin 19 jun 2018* advises;

- spend time in the shade between 11am and 3pm
- make sure you never burn
- cover up with suitable clothing and sunglasses
- take extra care with children
- use at least factor 15 sunscreen

On vitamin D, *nhs.uk* advises (paraphrased)

- that in spring and summer we can get enough vitamin D by spending time in the sun
- that in autumn and winter we are unlikely to get sufficient D from sunlight and should supplement with Vit D, or get it from our diet by eating foods such as oily fish, red meat, liver, egg yolks
- the recommended daily dose of Vit D is 10 microgram or 400 International Units (IU)
- do not take too much, more than 100 micrograms is harmful (50 for children)
- people with dark skins and those who work indoors all day should consider taking Vit D all year

TS (*the Diet Myth*) suggests that sunshine and oily fish are better than Vit D; he recommends 10-15 minutes sunshine on face and arms every day, and that if you do supplement, the preferred form of the vitamin is D3.

If you make a mistake and get too much sun the author has personally found Aloe Vera gel very good for treating burns including sunburn. Most sources say that its SPF is too low to use as a sunscreen, others indicate that it can absorb some UV.

B 9 Choose to Learn and Teach

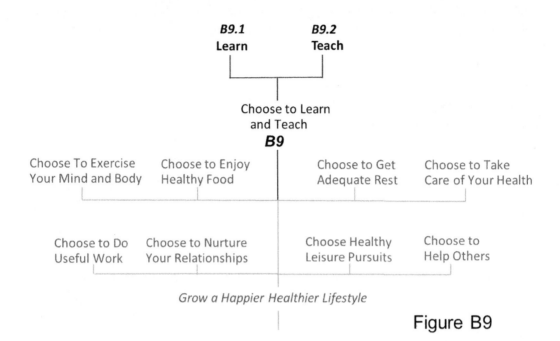

Figure B9

B 9 1 Learn

Learning not only can enrich us with a useful new skill, but it is also beneficial and uplifting. We enjoy encountering something new, and it helps broaden and refresh our mind. We also get the feeling of having achieved something when we master a new skill. Think of learning as a *lifelong process,* you are never too old to learn. It doesn't have to be a major enterprise, just as long as you continue to keep your mind open to learning, even small everyday things count.

You might choose to enroll on a course at a college or night school or join a local group. Or you might start a small individual project learning about something that interests you, or that you are curious about.

There has never been such a good time for learning. Apart from books and DVD or online courses, there is a wealth of material available online immediately through your browser, including books, dictionaries, websites, blogs and videos. In just seconds you can use your browser to get answers to satisfy your curiosity about any topic, or help you understand some difficult aspect that you've been struggling to understand. You can also get apps that help you learn and practice, for example, learning a language.

You can also learn by choosing new experiences when you get the opportunity. This can include experiencing new places, new activities, new people.

You could choose to start by learning one of the many beneficial practices suggested here (meditation, mindfulness, yoga, keep fit, nutrition etc.) so you get a multiple benefit.

B9.2 Teach

If you teach others useful skills, or knowledge that they want to receive, then this has two benefits. They gain in ability, and you get a good feeling of having helped them. This can happen in many small ways. For example, when you teach your children to behave well. You may teach younger members of your extended family or younger colleagues at work. You may teach by giving advice. Or it could be your vocation. You may also find that teaching may cause you to question the truth of what you've learned or cause you to think of the better ways to explain it. What you teach is part of your legacy. In Buddhism, teaching is given great merit.

Part 5 How to Use this Book

5.1 Making a Start

Everyone's approach will be different, but here are some suggestions to consider:

A good start would be to read the book right through, even if only a quick read. This will give you an overview of the whole subject, and the way the book is structured.

It may also give you an awareness of how complex the subject is. There's a lot to take in, and the topics seem to be all inter-related. This can be enough to make your head spin. But you can always go back to study and digest, in slower time, the information that most interests you.

Reading and digesting the book won't, in itself, make you any happier. It may, however, cause you think about some things that you don't normally stop to consider. It may also make you more aware of the *many diverse factors that can positively influence your happiness and your health*, and that's a useful start.

Its also possible that some of the ideas may permeate into your mind and have some gradual influence on your choices subsequently.

This awareness of the benefits that might be achievable may trigger in you a resolve to make some positive changes. It may be immediately clear to you where you want to start, but if not, some suggestions have been provided below that might help you decide.

5.2 Assess Your Thinking Patterns

Assess your own thinking and behaviour patterns against the "Happiness Tree" model. Do you recognize any good or bad personal traits? Are there things you'd like to change? Also assess your own "Happiness Cup". Has it got leaks that you can identify? Which taps are on? These assessments might lead you to choose specific areas that you want to focus on and change. Take your time to mull these things over, there's no rush. You might want to ask those close to you, they may see things that you can't. You might decide to team up with a friend and help each other.

5.3 Changing Your Thinking Patterns

For many people a good start would be to learn to meditate because this is said to help us make the other positive changes to our thinking traits and habits. You might also choose to learn some of the other mindfulness and positive thinking exercises (UR1). Whichever you choose, try and fix them into your daily routine. Initial guidance on how to do them is given in this book. It would be a great advantage to learn from an experienced teacher if you can, but if not, there are many other resources to help you on your way (books, DVD's, courses, retreats, online sources, YouTube, apps, groups). You need to persevere with these activities and allow time for them to have effect. Helping others, on the other hand, is something you can start straight away.

After you have started your meditation and mindfulness practice, when you are ready, select another thinking pattern topic that you want to work on. After you've followed the initial guidance given in this book you may want to study one specific aspect in more detail. You could find a specialist book or enroll on a course. Alternatively, you could choose some key words to describe what you want to achieve (for example *increase my self-esteem* or *learn to accept other people*) then search using your browser and tap into the wealth of more detailed resources and training techniques that are available online to help you progress.

5.4 Assess Your Lifestyle

Getting a Balance

We need some balance in our lifestyle, just as the branches of a tree need to be balanced. For example, some of us may tend to work too much and not spend enough time with family or in play. Others may tend to want to play all the time. Some of us get fixed on one activity to the exclusion of all others. Some of us spend too much time ruminating because were not sufficiently occupied. Others spend too much time alone. Look at your lifestyle and see if you need to rebalance it.

Routine

You may want to assess the level of routine in your lifestyle and see if you have a balance. Some level of routine is helpful in enabling to get on with jobs and avoid procrastinating. It can help us persevere with boring but important long-term tasks and help us schedule important leisure pastimes like exercise and meditation. But if we are a slave to routine, we may miss out on opportunities to try something new.

Variety

When you assess your lifestyle, you may decide that your tree is too uniform. You may want to add a new branch or sub-branch to give you more variety and contrast so that you are refreshed when you switch from one activity to another. Remember the saying: *"variety is the spice of life".*

5.5 Changing Your Lifestyle

Don't try to make too many major changes all at once, because major changes can cause stress. Take your time. Think instead of grafting or growing the shoots of new branches and pruning others. New branches of a tree take time to grow.

Don't expect to do everything, you won't have time. You're not trying to build a perfect lifestyle. There's no scoring here, it's about trying things and finding out what makes you happier, then continuing anything that works. Success will encourage you to try more. If you try something and it doesn't work, choose something else instead.

You might want to pick just one thing that would be particularly beneficial and start to implement it. You could choose an activity that gives multiple benefits. For example, going for a walk in a beautiful place with a friend gives you exercise, fresh air, uplifts you, gives you social contact and engages your mind. Joining a Yoga class engages you in learning and social contact, but also delivers health benefits of physical exercise and mental wellbeing. Learning to cook healthy food could become both a hobby, a study and a positive step to better health.

You may choose to try something you've always wanted to do but never got round to. Or something you've never plucked up the courage to try. You could team up with friends to try something new. Or join in something that your friends already do. You may be totally surprised and enjoy things that you previously thought were "not your cup of tea".

You may find that when you are open to change, an opportunity just turns up, and you can grasp it.

There may be times in your life when it's easier to make major changes because you are forced to by events beyond your control, like losing your job. Then be an opportunist and make the major change to do something better.

Similarly, there may be times in life when an exciting opportunity or adventure presents itself and you just have to take the plunge and change everything.

5.6 Your Multifold Path
Bear in mind this book doesn't suggest a quick fix, nor that you need to do everything at once. That might be overwhelming. Just making one or two changes at a time may give you a worthwhile benefit.

This book does not present happiness as a destination, but as a journey. You may like to think of it as a Multifold Path (like the Buddha's Eightfold Path) which has many strands to it, like a cable, as shown in Figure 5.1. As you travel along this path you try gradually, step by step, to cultivate your mind and develop your lifestyle, so that you learn to live each day a little more happily and healthily.

Your Multifold Path

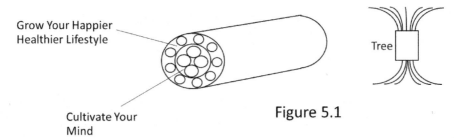

Figure 5.1

Some changes are harder to make than others, so include some easy and pleasant ones that you *want* to try. When making the more difficult changes you may not always find it an easy journey, but you can start with a few small steps. Even small changes bring benefits, and the pace is up to you, you have your whole life ahead of you.

Don't be put off if you don't get instant success. Learn from mistakes and reinforce success. If you struggle with applying any particular aspect of the process, remember that there is a wealth of further resources out there to help you. You could of course team up with a friend on your journey or join a group.

Part 6 Summary and Conclusions

Summary

The author has examined a wide range of sources to see what he could learn about the factors that influence our happiness and our health.

This search, being motivated by personal interest and curiosity, was not rigorous or scholarly. In some places it only scratched the surface. It did however draw from some authoritative sources, and it did span a wide range of disciplines.

It also covered a very wide time span running from our ape like ancestors, through traditions and philosophies from early history, right up to the scientific findings of modern research.

The author found it helpful to examine each subject in the context of the bigger picture that began to emerge.

The author drew his own personal conclusions, which are summarised below.

Conclusions

There are very many factors that affect our happiness and health, they are often interconnected.

The mind and body are very closely connected, so too are happiness and health.

There are some common themes that emerge from very different specialist fields of study. It is a complex and 'joined up' subject.

Some factors are more straightforward and easier to grasp than others, and some are not at all intuitive.

Some of the resulting implications are surprising, some are contentious, and. some, but not all, are supported by scientific evidence.

For example, modern science has revealed that the *microbiome* has a surprisingly important influence on our happiness and health. Also, that our brain is *plastic*. No doubt there will be more such revelations.

Human creativity and adaptability has enabled enormous progress to be made since the beginning of farming and the dawn of civilization. This has brought massive advantages. It has increased our material wealth, comfort and benefitted many other aspects of our everyday life. Medical science continues to make advances in curing our diseases, reducing our suffering, and keeping us alive for longer.

In contrast, some other consequences of our progress may be having a negative impact. Recent changes to our environment and lifestyles mean that many populations no longer live in the way that evolution formed us to. There seems to be a *mismatch* between the way we lived during our million years or so of evolution and the way many of us live now. Some aspects of this mismatch may be negatively influencing our happiness, as well as our physical and mental health.

That same human creativity is now enabling us to explore solutions to this problem. Many recommendations now widely advocated (such as exercising, reducing stress, eating a natural diet, and getting out of doors) could be viewed as measures that reduce the impact of this evolutionary *mismatch*.

Many factors in our lives, (such as pleasures, good relationships, and work satisfaction) have a positive effect on us and can be viewed as sources of happiness (*taps*).

Other factors (such as negative thought processes, and negative traits that can arise from our conditioning), can have a negative effect; they drain our happiness (*holes*), though we may not be aware of it.

The way these factors (taps and holes) influence our resulting level of happiness is depicted in the Happiness Cup Model.

We can learn a lot about the negative effects (holes) from some traditional teachings, as well as solutions that counter them. Modern science also provides solutions, (some of which appear to be consistent with the traditional methods).

Science suggests that about 50-60% of our happiness is determined by our genes. The rest we can influence by our thoughts, actions and lifestyle choices. Science also shows that lifestyle factors have a large influence on our health.

That's good news because it tells us that, for those who want to, there's plenty of scope for improving both our happiness and our health, by learning to make positive choices.

The author has attempted to summarise the many diverse factors which affect our happiness and health in the *Happiness Tree Model.* The model also shows the many positive choices that you can make, and how to implement them.

These diverse positive choices seem to share a common theme; they can all be viewed as ways of helping us to better '*match*' our mindset and lifestyle with the genetic inheritance provided to us by evolution.

For those readers who decide to make some changes, advice is provided here to help get you started.

The author also concludes that, given the importance of our happiness and our health, it is perhaps surprising that most of us don't learn a little more about the subject as part of our general education? On the other hand, he recognises the inherent difficulty involved; we already have too many other important things to learn.

Afterword

About the Author
The author was born in, England in 1944. He graduated at Exeter University where he was awarded a PhD in Physics in 1970. He then worked as a research physicist at Warwick University then at Ecole Polytechnique Federale de Lausanne in Switzerland. On returning to the UK, he switched to an engineering career, working for Marconi GEC, later BAE Systems. He developed an expertise in 'system engineering' on multidiscipline projects and was awarded the *GEC Prize for Individual Achievement* for developing a teaching model of *'System Engineering'* which was adopted company wide. He then taught this model in house, and as a visiting lecturer at the GEC Management College Dunchurch, and on MSc courses run by London and Loughborough Universities. He later spent a period of time as a self-employed inventor. He and his wife live in the UK, but also spend time each year with her family in Thailand.

The Origins of This Work
The author has long indulged his curiosity about 'how things work' and how new solutions can be found. He has long enjoyed the benefits of outdoor leisure and sport pursuits in countering a 'sedentary lifestyle' and 'too much thinking'. He has a long-held interest in human origins. During a period of ill health, he developed an interest in the effects of diet and lifestyle on health. During a period of unhappiness, he started to read a little about approaches to resolving unhappiness. More recently time spent in rural Thailand showed him at first hand that many people achieve happiness despite living with extreme poverty, hardship, and insecurity. It also resulted in the opportunity to read a little about Buddhism, to observe life in a Buddhist village and by chance to have a fascinating conversation one day with a German Buddhist monk called Daniel who was passing by on pilgrimage across Thailand (and who subsequently sent the author some books to read, for which the author remains very grateful). The author started to learn a little more, though he found some of the concepts of Buddhism, Mindfulness and the subject of happiness difficult to grasp.

He started reading more, making notes and thinking about links to lifestyle, evolution and psychology. His notes seemed very jumbled up like a *bowl of spaghettii*. They lacked structure. He began to wonder if his previous experience of making a teaching model could help him remedy this. Partitioning a system of complex information into a simple structure is never easy. There are many possible options; none are perfect, but some are better than others. He wanted to find a structure that is simple, that groups together conceptually similar things, that is easy to understand and remember, that is self- consistent, without too much overlap, and is balanced. And it had to be a structure that can be matched to a picture.

The author started grouping his notes according to topic and found that he needed big paper charts, like family trees, stuck on the wall in order to see the whole picture. He couldn't, at first, reconcile the very different natures of some of the topics that made up these *roots*. One day he turned some of them upside down and they became the *branches* and that improved things. He couldn't at first find a suitable way to split the remaining roots into suitable topics without overlaps or omissions, nor a suitable terminology for the headings. Eventually he found that the subdivisions *thought, action, reaction,* and *interaction* seemed to work better than others he had tried. He also decided to maximise the use of the words *learn* and *choose* because they are crucial to any self- help process. After a few more years, many iterations, pauses and doubts, the present *Happiness Tree* structure emerged. It is not perfect, but after many iterations and false starts the author finally feels that it meets the intended aims well enough.

After subsequent problems trying to disentangle and structure the many threads and apparent contradictions regarding the subject of happiness, the *Happiness Cup* model later followed. After a few more years work, with feedback and encouragement from friends, the book started to come together in its present form. More recently, after a further period of work trying to understand some of the more f*uzzy* aspects of our thinking, the *Mind State* model was added.

In any work such as this, there will doubtless be some errors and omissions. On some of the more contentious subjects dealt with, there will also remain differing views. In addition, science will continue to reveal more. The author regards this book as unfinished business, but feels that he has learned a lot on this journey. He hopes that he can succeed in sharing some of that with you. As a relative beginner, he doesn't claim to have implemented or tested all the many ideas presented here, but he has benefited from some at least, and intends to try more.

The Justification for This Book

Over the ages, many monks, teachers, scholars, doctors, and scientists have devoted their entire lives to developing and testing in depth the various branches of specialist knowledge that we touch on here. You may think it impertinent for a non-expert, who has only skimmed the surface by reading a few books, and not studied the subjects in great depth, to produce a summary in the way that the author has attempted. On the other hand, you might say that:

- it's worth a try, because if the aim could be achieved then it would be very useful to many people
- even if only partially successful the material could be progressively improved with more expert help (the structure lends itself to modular improvement, pinpointing errors or omissions and remedying them)
- the result, though imperfect, might be sufficiently good to encourage and sign post the reader to more detailed, more authentic sources of specific interest (acting as a map for the journey)
- the picture analogies, though imperfect may help understanding.

Some might say that the Buddhas teachings are complete and perfect as they stand and there is no need to represent them in a different way or add to them. There is truth in that. We are after all the same humans now as then, and his insights were so profound that they have stood the test of time. On the other hand, our health and wellbeing are now under threat in some new ways due to our lifestyle (factors such as plentiful but poor diet, lack of exercise, overworking, stress etc.). These factors are linked to obesity, diabetes, heart disease, depression and more. Health contributes to our sense of well-being. The Buddha once said that it was *our greatest gift.* It seems not illogical therefore to put *health* in the same model as *happiness.* Also, our *lifestyle* provides some of our sources of our happiness (achievement, job satisfaction, having fun, relationships etc.) and so deserves its place in any model of happiness. Another factor is that our pollution of the planet has increased dramatically in the last few hundred years, therefore, in this model, *conservation* is added to the section dealing with morals.

There are already hundreds of books, websites and videos out there covering Buddhism, Mindfulness, Nutrition, Exercise and the other subjects dealt with here, so you could say that we don't need *yet another one.* That also is true. On the other hand, if the presentation format used here could help the non-expert to understand the subject better, and if it could bring together relevant diverse material into one accessible place, and if it could act as a sort of grid map of the subject, then that might be considered justification. After all, the messages were never more relevant than now. The World Health Organisation has warned that mental illness will be the biggest global burden of disease by 2030.

Our minds and bodies are very complex. Any work such as this can raise as many philosophical questions as it answers. We know that ideas come and go. Is this model based on *truth* or is it just part of another *hyped fashion trend*? As you read this book, you will see that the author has referred (albeit not in an academically rigorous way) to scientific evidence that supports *some* of the ideas presented here (for example; the benefits of meditation and exercise, the mind body connection, the effects of stress and diet on health, and the evidence of our evolutionary past). For some other aspects, especially those relating to traditional techniques, there is less scientific evidence. On the other hand, some of these techniques have been written down, taught and practised continuously for two thousand years or more. Some of them are used by present day therapists who say, based on long experience, that they work. This may, despite the lack of evidence, persuade you to give them a try and find out for yourself if they are *"true"* in practice for you.

Resources

The author has provided this list for those who want to explore further. The author has not read them all and so is not in a position to endorse them all: You will have to judge for yourself which ones may be useful to you.

Human Evolution and Anthropology
Yuval Noah Harari *Sapiens: A Brief History of Humankind*
James Susman *Affluence Without Abundance*
Herman Pontzer *Burn*

Buddhism and Mindfulness
Buddhist quotes: *realbuddhaquotes.com, sourcesofinsight.com, goodreads.com,*
Thanissaro Bhikku *The Bhudda's Teachings, An Introduction*
Ajahn Jayasaro *Without and Within,*and *From heart and hand.* These books and several more are available free from jayassaro.panyaprateep.org and www.bia.or.th. There are also many podcasts and youtube videos (search jayasaro).
Ajahn Jayasaro's book *Without and Within* also provided the following list of websites and books. The first 3 on the list offer free eBooks.

> Buddhanet.org
> Accesstoinsight.org
> Forestsanghapublications.org
> Buddhistteachings.org
> Suanmokkh.org
> Bia.or.th
> Wanderingdhamma.org
> Buddhistchannel.tv
> Blogs.dickinson.edu/buddhistethics
> All books by Bhikkhu P.A.Payutto
> The Life of the Buddha by Bikkhu Nyanamoli
> The Great Disciples of the Buddha by Helmut Hecker
> The Foundations of Buddhism by Rupert Gethin
> Buddhist Religions by Robinson/Jordan/Thanissaro
> The Middle Length, Connected, and Numerical Discourses of the Buddha translated by Bikkhu Bodhi, and The Long Discourses of the Buddha translated by Maurice Walshe.
> Works by the Thai Masters eg Ajahn Maha Bua, Ajahn Cha, Ajahn Buddhasa are available for free download as are those of leading Western monks such as Ajahn Sumedho and Ajahn Thanissaro Bhikkhu

Prof Mark. W. Muesse *'Practising Mindfulness : An Introduction to Meditation'* (see *The Great Courses*). The Handbook that comes with this CD course provides an extensive bibliography. Here is just an extract;

> Stephen Batchelor *Buddhism Without Beliefs; a Contemporary Guide to Awakening*

Bhikkhu Bodhi *The Noble Eightfold Path; Way to the End of Suffering*
Boston Wisdom Publications *Mindfulness in Plain English*
R Hanson and R Mendius *Buddhas Brain; the Practical Neuroscience of Happiness, Love and Wisdom*
Rahula Walpola *What the Buddha Taught*
Matthieu Ricard *The Art of Meditation*
Jon Kabat-Zinn has written many books, these are some of the best known
Full Catastrophe Living, Wherever You Go There You Are
Coming to Our Senses
Mindfulness for Beginners
The Mindful Way Through Depression
Mindfulness Based Stress Reduction
You can also view his YouTube instructional videos for example on the Body Scan Technique.
Eckhart Tolle is the author of over sixty books including
The Power of Now
A New Earth
Living a Life of Inner Peace
Oneness With All Life
Stillness Speaks
He also produced many recordings YouTube videos and DVDs and set up *Erchardt Tolle Teachings* and *Eckhardttolle.com*
Shannon Harvey is a health journalist and author. She enlisted the help of scientists to put meditation to the test by trying it herself for one year and measuring what happened. Her books and other work include
My Year of Living Mindfully
The Whole Health Life
https://www.myyearoflivingmindfully.com/
https://www shannonharvey.com. This blog gives lots of information for beginners, particularly how to persevere with meditaion, and lists a wide range of useful resources such as books, apps, training centres and trainers.
https://www theconnection.tv is a DVD about the connection between the mind and the body, based on interviews with prominent scientists in the field.
The many organisations researching mindfulness include
The Oxford Mindfulness Centre (UK)
The Mindfulness Center Brown University, and The Centre for Investigating Healthy Minds (USA)
Openground and Monash University (AUS)

Psychology

Maslow 1943 *A Theory of Human Motivation*
Mihaly Csikszentmihalyi 1990 *Flow; the Psychology of Optimal Experience*
Martin Seligman 2002 *Authentic Happiness.*

Ed Diener *Culture and Wellbeing*, and *The Science of Wellbeing* plus hundreds of scientific papers available as *collected works*.

Happiness

Dalai Lama. *The Art of Happiness*, and *the Big Book of Happiness*

Amit Sood *The Mayo Clinic Handbook for Happiness*

Pursuit-of-happiness.org is exploring the benefits for education that arise from the Positive Psychology and Science of Happiness movements

Actionforhappiness.org. This global, UK based charity, aims to help people take practical steps to build a happier society

Projecthappiness.org is a global charity that aims to empower people to create greater happiness within themselves and the world

Global Happiness Organisation GHO is a non-profit organisation that aims to increase net happiness worldwide and to get a happiness agenda into mainstream politics

The World Happiness Report, published every year polls comparative levels of happiness in countries across the world. It uses the Gallup World Poll's measurement tools to do this. https:// worldhappiness.report

Thehappinessresearchinstitute.com is an independent think tank that explores why some societies are happier than others and informs decision makers, so as to improve the quality of life for citizens across the world.

Health, Nutrition, Herbs, Supplements

Some useful general websites

> *nia.nih.gov.>health* can help you identify reputable health websites
> The author has also used;
>> *nhs.uk, webMD, healthline.com, mayoclinic.com,*
>> *chriswoollamshealthwatch.com, canceractive.com*

Prof Tim Sector *the Diet Myth, the Real Science Behind What We Eat*

Chris Woolams has written some valuable health related books including

> *Everything You Need to Know to Beat Cancer*
> *The Rainbow Diet and How it Can Help You Beat Cancer*
> *Rainbow Recipes*
> *Heal Your Gut Heal Your Body*
> *Oestrogen, The Killer In Our Midst*
> His charity websites *canceractive.com* and *chriswoollamshealthwatch.com* and his associated *Newsletter* are a valuable source of information on health and on the results of the latest research findings

Dr Nicholas Culpeper *The Complete Herbal*

Dr James A Duke *The Green Pharmacy* and *Anti Ageing Prescriptions*.

L White and S Foster *The Herbal DrugStore*

Julia Hill *the Mood Cure* and *the Diet Cure*

Dale Pinnock *Anxiety and Depression Eat Your Way to Better Health*, also *The Medicinal Chef: Eat Your Way to Better Health*

Jean Carper *Food Your Miracle Medicine*

Emily Jane's *Back to Natural Eating*
Patrick Holford *The Optimum Nutrition Bible,* and *the Holford Diet*
the Editors of Rodale Press *Healing with Vitamins and Minerals,*
The Readers Digest *Guide to Vitamins Minerals and Supplements,*
Dr Richard Firshein *The Nutraceutical Revolution*

Mind Body Exercise
Christina Brown The Book of Yoga
Dr Paul Liam MD *Teaching Tai Chi Effectively* and *Overcoming Arthritis*. Also, many DVDs and some free YouTube lessons.

Technology
There are many Apps available to help you meditate
There are many other online resources such as training courses and videos
The are some biofeedback devices that can help you with relaxation sleep and meditation.

Appendix 1 The Mind State Model

A1 Introduction

Although our minds are hugely complex, according to Amit Sood MD *(The Mayo Clinic Handbook for Happiness)*, we can simplistically think of it as having only two states, *'engaged'* or *'disengaged'*.

Psychiatrist Dr Dan Siegel *(Aware, the Science and Practise of Presence*, and *garrisoninstitute.com)* created a picture model called the *Wheel of Awareness* to explore awareness and consciousness. He used it extensively in Psychotherapy. The model depicts a *Rim* around which are distributed our 5 senses, our body sensations, our mental activities and our connections to others and to the world. The *Hub* represents our awareness and the *Spoke* our attention to the topics on the *Rim*.

The author has taken his useful model and modified it so as to visually depict, and explore in more detail, the particular mind states of *engagement* and *disengagement* discussed by Amit Sood. A particular aim initially was to visually represent the disengaged *monkey mind* state, but it was then extended further.

The resulting *Mind State Model* is explained below, and the theme gradually developed with the aid of a series of diagrams.

Caveat This model is exploratory and still evolving. It's just an idea by the author to see if he can imagine a visual model that helps promote understanding of this particular subject. It is not based on any evidence or science or pre-existing models (other than the two quoted above). It has not been reviewed or tested so it may be invalid. For that reason, it has been put separately in this Appendix, so as not to disrupt the flow of the main body of text, (which is separate from, and independent of this model). In this first attempt the model does not address how we process sound, nor the detail of what processing goes on inside the tube and outside of it.

A2 Overview of the Model

Figure A1 shows a hollow ball or sphere with three round holes in its surface. Inside the ball is an open-ended tube that rotates in the vertical plane about a horizontal axis (think of a toilet roll tube inside a plastic toy ball, the roll has been skewered on a kebab stick, but is free to rotate on the stick, like a wheel on an axle, to align with one of the holes).

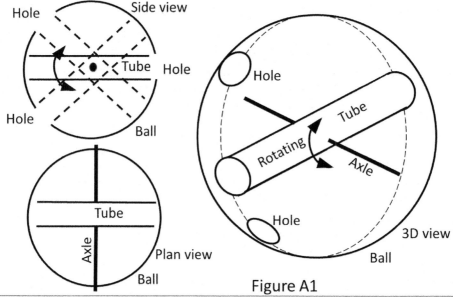

Figure A1

Imagine a clear plastic hollow ball with 3 round holes in its surface. Inside the ball is an open ended tube that rotates about a horizontal axle so that the ends of the tube can line up with the holes.

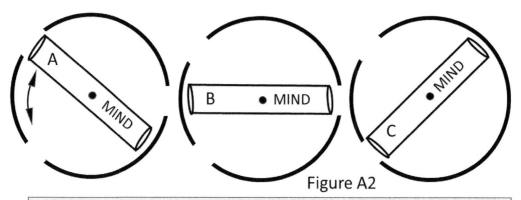

Figure A2

Inside the ball, the open ended tube contains our **mind**. The tube *rotates* to and fro between three positions A, B, C as our **mind** shifts its *focus of attention*. In each position one end of the tube aligns with one of the holes. The mind receives information through the holes.

Figure A2 shows our **mind** as being located inside the tube. The sphere can be thought of as our *head* or *brain*. The tube rotates to and fro between three positions A, B, C as our mind *shifts its focus of attention*. In each position one end of the tube aligns with one of the holes in the sphere, through which it receives information. The tube can be in only one position at a time, but it can flip rapidly to and fro between them.

A3 Our Mind Focused on the Outside World (Engaged State)

Figure A.3 shows our external and internal sensors located on the outside of the sphere, accessed by two of the holes. They send signals into the tube when it is suitably aligned. These signals are represented by the arrows. The ends of the tube acts as a sort of funnel channelling these signals into the mind. This is the only access that our mind has to the outside world and to body sensations. It generates perceptions and thoughts in the tube in response to these incoming signals. Outside of the sphere on the left side, is the real world, monitored by our sensors. On the right side is our imaginary world which can only be accessed when the reverse end of the tube is aligned with the third hole. Each position of the tube is explained in more detail below.

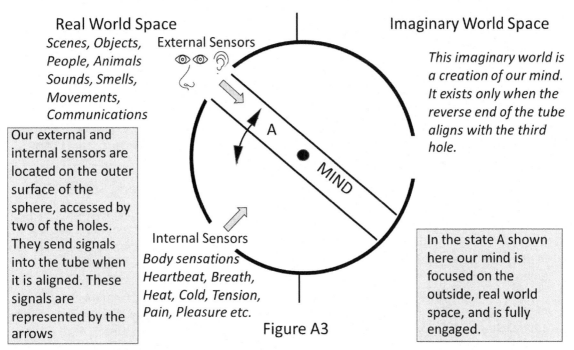

Real World Space
Scenes, Objects, People, Animals Sounds, Smells, Movements, Communications

External Sensors

Imaginary World Space

This imaginary world is a creation of our mind. It exists only when the reverse end of the tube aligns with the third hole.

Our external and internal sensors are located on the outer surface of the sphere, accessed by two of the holes. They send signals into the tube when it is aligned. These signals are represented by the arrows

A

MIND

Internal Sensors
Body sensations Heartbeat, Breath, Heat, Cold, Tension, Pain, Pleasure etc.

In the state A shown here our mind is focused on the outside, real world space, and is fully engaged.

Figure A3

In the mind state shown in Figure A3 our mind is focused on our external sensors. It is processing data from the world (sight, sound, smell, taste and touch). It is creating perceptions of the constantly changing world and deciding how to react to them. It is responding rapidly *in real time* without pausing to reflect; (the processes include those previously shown in Part1, Figure LR3.1). Its reactions include outgoing signals (not shown here). These could include, for example activating muscles, or releasing hormones, or initiating a mood change.

In this state our mind is fully attentive and engaged. It is not consciously attentive to our internal sensors and not using imagination. It carries out many of its tasks automatically, without much conscious thought, using learned behaviour and skills embedded subconsciously and in muscle memory. We are in this state for much of the time when working or playing or engaged in conversation, and we tend to be happy in this state.

A4 Our Mind in Reflective State (Engaged).

Sometimes, when we are engaged with the outside world we must pause to *reflect*, for example to find the answer to a question. This is depicted in Figure A4 below. by a *rotation* of the *tube* such that our mind has access to the *imaginary world space.* This imaginary world is entirely created and populated by our mind (inside the tube), but the author has found it helpful to draw it outside of the mind because that's how the mind *sees* it, as a *reflection* of the real world. This imaginary world space contains scenarios and images of objects drawn from memory of past events, represented by the outgoing arrow, and forms a *spatial reconstruction* of the real world, *a reflection* of it. The *imagined* objects can become modified, added to and rearranged by our thought processes so as to form *new objects* and *new scenarios.* These in turn provide *new inputs* to our mind (denoted by the ingoing arrow) provoking *new thoughts* in our mind. This process thus creates a feedback loop. The new thoughts from the imaginary world space have the same power to create emotions and reactions as those generated by the real world. They play an essential part in everyday life, and are especially important in gaining insight and understanding, in solving problems, making innovations and being creative. Our language recognises this ...*I see in my minds eye…turn the problem on its head…look at it a different way…it needs a fresh eye.* We can also use this facility to imagine future scenarios and make *predictions* of likely future outcomes.

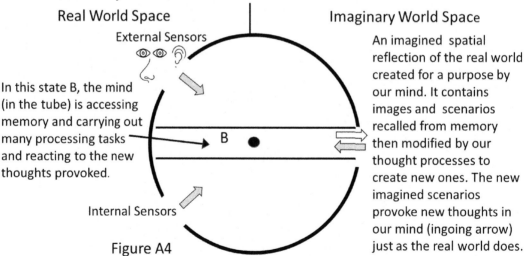

Figure A4

This picture represents mind state B, in which our mind is reflecting *with a purpose.* It is no longer focused on our sensors. It has paused to carry out *off line* processing before deciding how to react to the events previously detected. It remains fully engaged.

We could use another analogy; think of a mobile phone that has the screen reversed so it points inwards. Think of your mind as being inside the phone. You see the world looking forward, through the camera lens. You record it in memory, when you take a photo. Later, when you want to, you can stop looking through the lens reconstruct the image from memory and turn to view it on the screen, in slow time, to analyse it in more detail.

This imaginary world is not a perfect reflection of the real world, but it doesn't need to be, and it gives us other advantages instead. For example, our *'imaginary'* world is *'offline'*, it is not connected to time. If he tries to imagine a *galloping horse: the* author finds that he doesn't see a moving *video* but rather a series of *static freeze frame* images. On the other hand, you don't have to go to a racecourse you can imagine a galloping horse anywhere, at any time, and you can place it on the moon or running across a lake, such is the power of imagination. The fact that our imaginary world is not running in *real time* bestows a great advantage: It can take all the time that is needed to make a considered reaction or to solve a difficult problem.

The images in our imaginary world are probably not exact photographic replicas of the real world but symbolic, iconic representations almost like labels that we recognise (just as we recognise letters and numbers). Maybe they are in the same code as our recorded visual perceptions of the real world and maybe this saves processing time and memory requirement? Maybe that's also why our mind reacts to them as though they were from the real world?

When we are in this imaginary world, it is plausible that our mind, in the tube, is busy moving to and from memory and carrying out complex processing tasks. It might be asking questions (how, what, when, who, why), comparing, assessing, making deductions and decisions. In this state our mind is still *engaged in a purposeful activity* and is not easily distracted so it is *generally happy* (provided that we don't overwork it).

It seems that, for most of the time, only rational, logical, thoughts images and scenarios pass from our mind to our imaginary world: (this may arise from the fact that most of our stored memories are normal and rational). In this model we can represent this as a filter over the hole that leads to the imaginary world. We can, if we want to be creative, learn to remove this filter. Examples of this are Salvador Dali's *surrealist art*, and Edward de Bono's *Brainstorming* techniques such as turning an idea upside down or inside out.

Note that in this reflective state we may still have our eyes 'open' but we are not paying attention to the signals they are sending us. Interestingly when you ask someone a question, you may notice their eyes move upwards as their mind flips from one state to the other to find the answer. Or they may close their eyes to concentrate. Or you may see someone's eyes *glaze over* and focus on the distance, or they may say *umm*). Sometimes we stay in this reflective state for only a second or two before again attending to our sensors (as when someone asks us the date and we've temporarily forgotten). At other times we may be in this state for long periods trying to understand something or solve a problem. We can generate a train of thoughts one leading to another.

(As an aside it is interesting to conjecture how our mind *chooses* which way to point the tube. We are unlikely to enter reflective mode if we perceive an external threat and must react quickly, so we stay engaged. If we experience the external world to be interesting, pleasing, or entertaining or if it arouses our curiosity, or offers a prospect of reward then we are likely to remain engaged with the world. Similarly, if we get absorbed in purposeful and creative thinking we are not easily distracted. If we are in pain or discomfort or experiencing pleasure, we pay attention to our internal sensors. If none of these conditions apply, we get bored and inattentive, then it seems that we *default* to the monkey mind state, it's as though there's a spring pulling the tube to position B (see below). There is another controlling mechanism; when we are in reflection mode or disengaged or asleep, there is an alarm system that brings us back to reality very suddenly, for example if we hear a loud bang).

A5 The Disengaged Mind State

Figure A5 below represents the state when our mind is *disengaged.* The tube is in the same position as in the previous diagram, so our mind is not paying attention to our sensors and has access to the imaginary world. It has gone *offline*, but for no specific or immediate *purpose*. This seems to be the *default* condition when we are not occupied. In this state, while it is receiving no sensory input and has no directions, our mind generates *uninvited* images and thoughts apparently at random from memory (outgoing arrow). These images generate more thoughts in response (ingoing arrow).

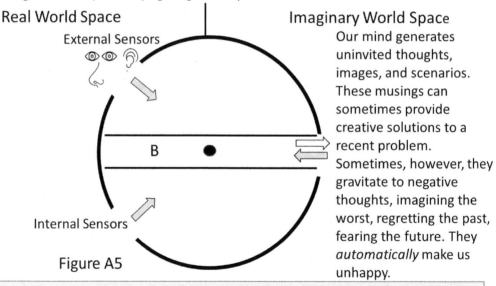

Real World Space

External Sensors

Imaginary World Space

Our mind generates uninvited thoughts, images, and scenarios. These musings can sometimes provide creative solutions to a recent problem. Sometimes, however, they gravitate to negative thoughts, imagining the worst, regretting the past, fearing the future. They *automatically* make us unhappy.

B

Internal Sensors

Figure A5

This picture the represents the state when our mind is ***disengaged***. It has gone off line, but *not deliberately,* and for *no particular purpose.* This *monkey mind* state seems to be the default mode when we are not occupied.

It's possible that these images and thoughts are not actually *random.* It may be that our subconscious mind *preferentially* offers up images and thoughts relating to topics that we have previously, recently, been thinking about (in a similar way that your *phone's browser* learns your preferences and offers you material that *'it thinks'* you will be interested in).

For example, if you've recently been trying to solve a complex problem, or create something new, it may be that you have to address and reflect on many different aspects of the problem, and possible solutions, until they are all in this *'preferential'* category of memory. Only then can you *'get your brain round'* the problem. You are then able to muster all the relevant data together, at the same time, in your imagination (rather than having to look sequentially and more slowly, possibly into deeper memory). In this situation these uninvited musings may sometimes be very helpful or even creative. They may suddenly deliver a new insight or new idea that you can develop into a solution.

However, if you have recently been thinking about some negative aspect of your life, particularly something that has no obvious solution, then this same process can work *against* you. Your uninvited thoughts then gravitate towards being negative, and they automatically trigger negative feelings that make you unhappy. You can become *lost* in these thoughts for long periods of time, but unaware of it. You are no longer in control of your mind, *"it"* has taken control of *"you"*. Worse still, these negative thoughts can create a positive feedback loop; the more you think about them, the more your mind treats them as preferred thoughts, so they become more and more reinforced and keep coming back to haunt you. It's as though repetition makes them more embedded; they become like a railway track that goes on a set journey round various loops. Each trip makes your mood lower, but you may find it hard to get off the track to go somewhere else.

We normally don't give much consideration to how our mind works, so we're not conscious of how these uninvited thoughts are constantly making us unhappy, yet they can be the biggest source of our unhappiness. They were likened by the Buddha to a monkey jumping around the branches of a tree *(the monkey mind)*. If we are to become happier, we have to find a way to break the loop. We have already discussed in *UR1* and *UR2* above various ways to counter this problem; for instance by a suitable distraction activity, or by finding ways to disarm or replace the negative thought.

A6 Paying Attention to Our Internal Sensors

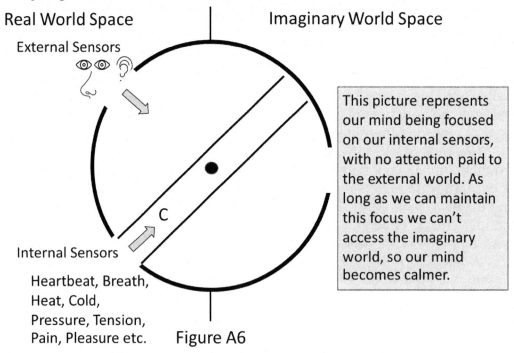

Real World Space | Imaginary World Space

External Sensors

Internal Sensors

Heartbeat, Breath,
Heat, Cold,
Pressure, Tension,
Pain, Pleasure etc.

This picture represents our mind being focused on our internal sensors, with no attention paid to the external world. As long as we can maintain this focus we can't access the imaginary world, so our mind becomes calmer.

Figure A6

Figure A6 represents our mind being focused on our internal sensors (nerves sensing heat, cold, pressure etc.), with no attention paid to the external world and no access to the imaginary world. We don't normally spend much time in this mode unless we are experiencing pain or pleasure. As long as we can maintain the focus on our body's sensors, we can't access imaginary space so our mind remains engaged and can become *calm*.

Below in A7 -A10, we extend this mind state model to illustrate the meditation and mindfulness techniques previously described in UR1. The aim is to see if pictures can help us learn and understand the techniques more readily, or even provide insight as how they might work.

In A11 below we extend the model further in an attempt to describe the relaxation and the sleep cycle.

A7 Breath Meditation

A visual analogy of the breath meditation process is shown in Figure A7 below. When you have your attention consciously and fully focused on your breath, your *mind tube* is in position C. In this position your mind can't access the Imaginary World Space, so it can't wander. If you momentarily lose focus on the breath, the tube is on a spring and rotates back to the default position B allowing your mind to drift out into Imaginary World. It can stay there wandering around at random for some time before you become consciously aware of what's happened. You then must refocus attention on your breath to pull the tube back to position C. During a meditation session the tube will be repeatedly rotating between the two states C and B. You will be continually working against the spring to keep your tube in state C, and repeatedly becoming aware at some point that it has rotated to state B and repeatedly having to pull it back again.

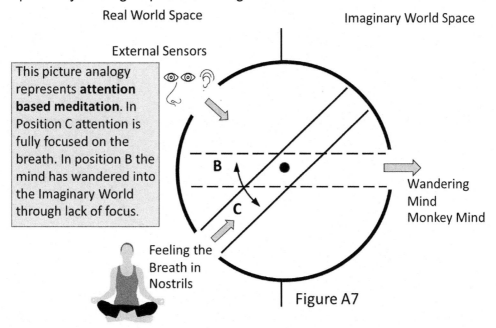

Figure A7

A8 Insight Meditation

A picture analogy of Insight Meditation is attempted in Figure A8 below.
Begin with attention-based breath meditation. Then, having calmed and cleared
your mind, move your attention away from the breath and focus attention on a
particular theme regarding the human condition and the nature of things. The
themes emphasised by the Buddha, were *Impermanence*, *Suffering* (the
unsatisfactory nature of life), and the concept of *Self*. Because your mind was
cleared of clutter by the breath meditation you may be able to see things more
clearly. You may also gain beneficial insight into the way that your mind works
and the way that it has been conditioned.

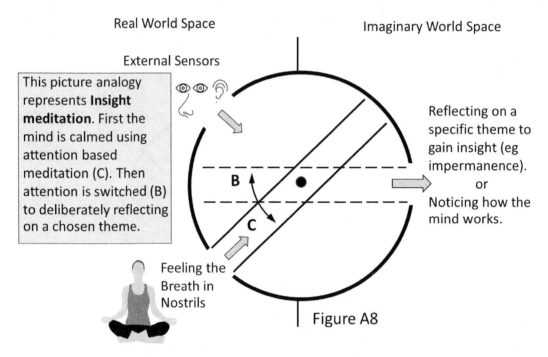

Figure A8

You can choose to reflect on other themes. For example, negative traits
and how we can detach from them; coping with grief or pain; how to be more
compassionate, or less angry, or how to reduce hatred.

A9 Bodyscan Meditation

Figure A9 below is a visual analogy to describe a Bodyscan Meditation. You have many *inner* sensors distributed throughout your body, constantly sending messages to your brain. The sensations you feel might arise from sensors in your skin, your scalp, your nerves, muscles, joints and inner organs. The sensations might include warmth or coolness, tension or lightness, pain or discomfort, contact pressure, pulsing, movement, sensitivity, numbness. tingling, itching, or moving air. You may feel no sensation in some areas, be aware of this as well.

Having got in position and relaxed you slowly scan down your whole body from the top of your head to the tips of your toes, paying attention to any sensations you feel in each area as it is scanned (think of a spotlight moving slowly down your body picking up the outputs of all your internal sensors).

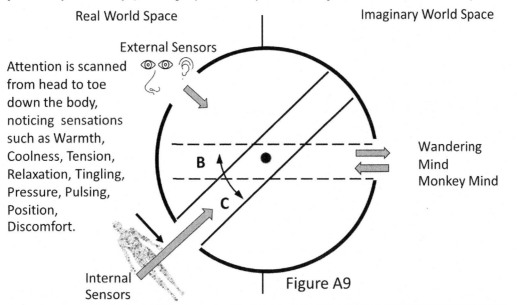

Figure A9

This picture analogy represents **attention based bodyscan meditation**. In Position A attention is fully focused on various internal sensors. In position B the mind has wandered into the Imaginary World through lack of attention.

Start with your scalp, focus on any sensations you can detect there. Notice the nature of the sensations, accept them without judging them as good or bad, then move onto the forehead and temples and note any sensations you can detect there.

Continue this process scanning in turn your eyes, nose, cheeks, mouth. Then scan your chin, jaw and ears. Then the back of your head, and the top of your neck and down to your shoulders. Move down to your upper arms, forearms, wrists, and hands. Then move to your chest, ribs, upper back and shoulder blades. When your attention wanders just bring it back to your body sensations.

Continue moving the spotlight down your spine and lower back, and abdomen, notice the movement due to your breath, and any sensation from your inner organs. Then progress down through your hips and groin, your thighs, knees, shins, calves, to your feet and toes.

Finally bring the scan to an end by feeling your whole body, relaxed and present in the moment.

A10 Mindfulness Exercises

We can use the model to visually represent a Mindfulness Exercise as shown in Figure A10. In state A our mind is fully *engaged* processing data from the outside world in real time and deciding how to react. We are in this state most of the time when working or playing or engaged in conversation.

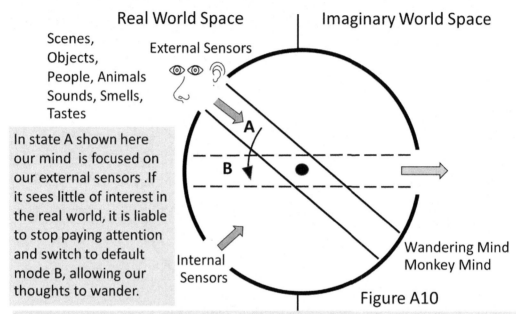

Real World Space | Imaginary World Space

Scenes, Objects, People, Animals Sounds, Smells, Tastes

External Sensors

In state A shown here our mind is focused on our external sensors .If it sees little of interest in the real world, it is liable to stop paying attention and switch to default mode B, allowing our thoughts to wander.

Internal Sensors

Wandering Mind Monkey Mind

Figure A10

By *Mindfully* paying attention to the details that we observe in the real world, even when we don't need to, we create extra interest that stops our mind switching from mode A to mode B.

However if our mind finds the scenario it is engaged with to be of insufficient interest then it stops paying attention, *disengages* and switches to default mode B, which allows our mind to wander into the imaginary world. For example, this is more likely to happen if we sense no threat or prospect of reward, or if we see nothing exciting or unusual to maintain our attention. However, if we deliberately, **mindfully**, choose to pay full attention to all the sensations that we are experiencing, **even though we don't need to**, then we may create enough interest, or pleasure, or notice new things, sufficient to delay our mind switching to default mode and producing negative thoughts. If we can learn to do this often in our everyday lives then we become less vulnerable to negative thinking. We may also learn to fully enjoy the present, rather than rushing on to the next activity.

A11 Relaxation and Sleep

Figure A11 is an attempt to visually represent the relaxation and sleep cycle. To do this we have introduced two new tube positions D and E and an extra hole that gives access to the same imaginary world that was shown in the previous diagrams. The objective is to see if we can visualise the sequence involved in relaxation and sleep (Note that brainwave frequencies and descriptions are approximate only; sources vary a little in the detail).

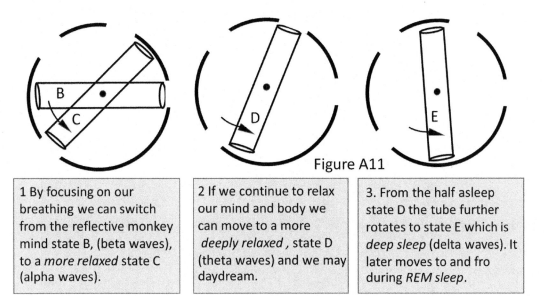

Figure A11

1 By focusing on our breathing we can switch from the reflective monkey mind state B, (beta waves), to a *more relaxed* state C (alpha waves).	2 If we continue to relax our mind and body we can move to a more *deeply relaxed*, state D (theta waves) and we may daydream.	3. From the half asleep state D the tube further rotates to state E which is *deep sleep* (delta waves). It later moves to and fro during *REM sleep*.

     The first stage of the diagram shows the transition from the 'eyes shut but wide awake' *reflecting* mode B to a *more relaxed* state C which we can achieve by relaxing our physical body and by focussing on our breath and shutting out our thoughts and worries of the day (calming our monkey mind). Our brainwave frequency drops from around 14-32 cps (Beta), to around 7-14 cps (Alpha) as we move from B to C.

     The second stage shows that if we continue with our calmed mind and relaxed body, the tube rotates further to position D, which is a *deeply relaxed* state. Our brainwave frequency drops to 4-7 cps (Theta). In this state our mind has access to the *imaginary world*, via the hole, and we may daydream. This half-awake state occurs just before sleep and before waking. The nature of what we dream is not always rational it can be surreal. (In this model we can think that there is not a *rational* filter on this hole).

     The third stage shows the transition from half asleep D to deep sleep E, where our brain frequency drops to 0.5- 4 cps (Delta). In this state our mind pays no attention to external or internal sensors and it has no access to the imaginary world. It is resting and is thought to be carrying out maintenance and consolidation tasks, such as storing in memory what we have learned during the day.

After a period of time, often quoted as 90 minutes, we move from deep sleep to REM (rapid eye movement sleep) in which we dream. The tube is probably moving to and fro between states. REM produces a mixture of Theta and Beta waves but also a high frequency wave denoted Gamma 32-100 cps.

During a night's sleep we may move from deep sleep to REM and back again many times before returning to half awake D, and finally, via C and B, to wide awake A.

Some sources suggest that expert meditators become able to more easily control the movement of the tube between the various mind state positions, and can more readily influence their brain wave frequency.

Printed in Great Britain
by Amazon

20695236R00095